VIRTUAL TRAINING

VIRTUAL TRAINING

THE ART OF CONDUCTING POWERFUL VIRTUAL
TRAINING THAT ENGAGES LEARNERS AND MAKES
KNOWLEDGE STICK

JEB BLOUNT

WILEY

Published by John Wiley & Sons, Inc., Hoboken, New Jersey.
Published simultaneously in Canada.

For general information on our other products and services or for technical support, please contact our Customer Care Department within the United States at (800) 762-2974, outside the United States at (317) 572-3993 or fax (317) 572-4002.

Wiley publishes in a variety of print and electronic formats and by print-on-demand. Some material included with standard print versions of this book may not be included in e-books or in print-on-demand. If this book refers to media such as a CD or DVD that is not included in the version you purchased, you may download this material at http://booksupport.wiley.com. For more information about Wiley products, visit www.wiley.com.

Library of Congress Cataloging-in-Publication Data is Available:
ISBN 9781119755838 (Hardcover)
ISBN 9781119755814 (ePDF)
ISBN 9781119755845 (ePub)

COVER DESIGN: PAUL MCCARTHY
COVER ART: © RAINBOW NIMA/SHUTTERSTOCK

SKY10026826_051721

Contents

Foreword

I'm the first to admit that I thought that in-person training was the only real way to teach people. I never imagined that I'd be delivering hundreds of hours of virtual training to audiences around the world from my virtual training studio on my farm in New Jersey.

But, as Jeb will share with you, our organization was forced to pivot fast in the spring of 2020 as the global pandemic raced around the globe. Our survival rested on my training team quickly embracing and mastering virtual training delivery.

It was not easy. Some of our trainers were in a momentary state of denial. But Jeb challenged us to adopt a new set of beliefs and think differently about virtual training. He pushed us out of our personal comfort zones. He demanded that we elevate our craft and deliver a legendary virtual learning experience.

My training team implemented and executed the exact techniques and tactics laid out in this book, and the results have been nothing short of remarkable. Mastering virtual instructor-led training has allowed us to scale faster, deliver more training, and make a massive and lasting impact on our clients' learners and their organizations.

More importantly, these techniques have made our master trainers better than they ever were before. We now seamlessly blend classroom-based training, virtual instructor-led training, and self-paced e-learning, in ways we never thought possible, to deliver a far higher ROI for our stakeholders.

An important and undeniable truth is that the organizations that continually train and develop their people build an unassailable competitive edge. These organizations are more agile, attract and retain top talent, and win. Within these "learning organizations," learning and development professionals are under constant pressure to source, develop, and deliver impactful training that is relevant, engaging, and sticks over the long haul. But you already know this, which is why you are reading this book.

It's likely that you picked this book up because you are seeking answers to the same pressing questions being asked by the leaders of forward-thinking organizations:

- How can we leverage virtual training to deliver more training, at a lower cost, while making an even bigger impact?
- How do we leverage virtual training to accelerate, elevate, and advance learning initiatives?
- How do we evolve as a learning and development organization and stay ahead of the curve?
- How do we make virtual training more engaging and impactful?
- How do I teach my trainers (or myself) to be comfortable delivering a high-quality experience in the virtual classroom?

In *Virtual Training*, Jeb Blount, who is one of the most celebrated trainers of our generation, answers these questions and delivers a blueprint for leveraging virtual instructor-led training to accelerate the velocity of learning initiatives and make training stick.

He gives you step-by-step instruction for leveraging technology, building virtual training sets, designing, and delivering engaging high-quality virtual training that learners and their leaders will embrace. You will learn the keys to future-proofing both yourself and your organization. Most importantly, you will learn how to elevate your craft and deliver a legendary virtual learning experience. I can tell you from first-hand experience that when you adopt and implement the techniques laid out in this book, you will begin making a far bigger impact than you ever thought possible, now and in the future.

This book matters because now, more than ever, we must think differently about the value of virtual instructor-led training and where it fits into broader learning initiatives. *Virtual Training* is a rare, transformational book that will reshape the way you and your organization view and deliver virtual instructor-led training forever.

—Keith Lubner,
Executive Vice President and
Head of Training & Consulting, Sales Gravy

Special Note: Free Virtual Training Resources

Virtual Training covers the fundamentals, which will likely remain constant, but it's impossible to include everything you need. The tools, technology, and trends in virtual training are constantly changing, so I created a place to keep you updated on the techniques that will give you an edge as you grow your virtual training skills.

The companion website to this book will keep you up to date and give you a place to dig into details about our favorite tools that we use at Sales Gravy, recommended apps, and other tips. As a special bonus to thank you for purchasing this book, you get free access to these resources.

Book passages that connect to additional website content are marked with this icon:

You can visit the companion website using this special, exclusive code, which will give you free access. Go to the following website and follow the instructions:

Web address: https://www.salesgravy.com/vt

Access code: VTB2021X

PART I

The Virtual Training Tsunami

The only way you survive is you continuously transform into something else.
—Gini Rometty, Executive Chairman of IBM

1 | Just Like That, Everything Changed

An instant wave of panic came over me as I grasped the gravity of the situation. The Covid-19 pandemic had made its way around the world.

Two days earlier, I'd delivered a keynote to 6,000 people. I didn't know it then, but it would be the last time I'd walk onto a physical stage or into a physical classroom for almost a year.

Before Covid, my training and consulting company, Sales Gravy, had been on a hyper-growth trajectory. Our master trainers were on the ground delivering training on every continent except Antarctica.

The year before, I'd spent 311 nights in hotel rooms, clocking over 200,000 air miles as I crisscrossed the globe delivering keynotes, workshops, and trainings to a who's who of the most prestigious organizations in the world.

With the economy on fire and our company growing at an ever-increasing pace, my trainers and I were road warriors. Our training calendar was packed, and my sales team was inundated with calls and emails from even more companies that wanted to hire us. I was getting regular inquiries from venture capital and private equity firms that wanted to discuss potential investments. It felt like we were unstoppable.

And then, just like that, everything changed. A global pandemic. Travel bans. Social distancing. Working from home. Panic. In a heartbeat, we were grounded.

Educators, instructors, and trainers were confronting a harsh reality. Classrooms were empty and livelihoods were on the line. It was chaos and we were in an all-hands-on-deck battle to save our company.

I remember sitting down with my company's CFO to figure out how long we could keep paying our trainers if we lost all of our training contracts. My number one focus was saving the business while retaining the talented people on our team that we'd worked so hard to attract and develop.

Meanwhile, customers were ringing our phones off the hook. Most of our scheduled trainings in physical classrooms were being indefinitely postponed. Our account executives were working to calm our panicked clients long enough to move those deliveries to the virtual classroom. As entire companies shifted from working together in office buildings to working from home, the organizations we served were frantically seeking alternatives to classroom learning.

In the midst of this initial shock wave, large companies were laying off members of their learning and development teams. Out-of-work corporate trainers were contacting us in droves. They were looking for advice, a shoulder to cry on, and, mostly, jobs.

The entire education, training, learning, and development industry was being forced to instantly pivot from classroom-based training to virtual training. And most trainers and organizations were woefully unprepared.

History is full of transformational points in which smart, innovative people were pressed to invent technology that could help them meet the moment, but at least for those of us in the training world, the powerful, high-quality technology was right in front of us. All we needed to do was catch up.

The Remote Learning Tidal Wave

In those early months, virtual training felt entirely new. Legions of trainers, disoriented and unsettled, approached virtual training as if they were stumbling into an alien world on some distant planet.

Remote learning, instruction, and training, though, is not new. Correspondence courses have been advertised in newspapers since the early 1700s, when the United States was still a colony. The earliest on record was for a course in shorthand, a style of notetaking, that was placed in the *Boston Gazette* in 1728.

It took until the 1920s for colleges to start broadcasting courses over the radio, and by the 1950s, some universities offered courses over broadcast television. Thanks to teleconferencing, in 1976, Coastline Community College in California became the first fully virtual institution.

Then, the internet arrived and brought remote learning into a new era. As corporate learning, development, and enablement started investing in new technologies, online courses became mainstream. I took my first virtual instructor-led course in the late 1990s. It leveraged an online content portal and weekly conference calls (audio only) with the instructor.

By the early twenty-first century, video conferencing technology was ubiquitous—and virtual instruction and e-learning technology exploded. Massive investment in online learning by corporate and governmental organizations accelerated innovation even more. Over the past 20 years, there has been a 900 percent market growth rate for online learning.[1]

But there was a problem: Most of the investment was focused on self-directed, asynchronous e-learning. Those types of courses aren't instructor-led—meaning, students log on whenever they want, consume preassigned content, and do some assignments that may or may not be graded or reviewed by anyone. Students and instructors often don't interact, and there's only a limited student community, if there's any at all.

Despite these drawbacks, venture capitalists and investors have poured money into e-learning companies, and some e-learning platforms were snapped up by bigger organizations. LinkedIn, for example, paid $1.5 billion for Lynda.com.[2]

In the online learning boom of the past two decades, there was a massive focus on asynchronous e-learning, while synchronous virtual instructor-led training (VILT) was mostly treated as an afterthought. Even with all of the investment and attention focused on e-learning, only 10 percent of synchronous training delivery was virtual.[3]

Don't get me wrong. Plenty of people and technology entrepreneurs were thinking about it. The problem was that, in learning and development (L&D), virtual training was more likely to be talked about than actually delivered. (It didn't help when the initial excitement about massive open online courses (MOOCs) fizzled with a 94 percent abandonment rate.)[4]

My company was one of the few that had been delivering VILT programs since 2011. These deliveries almost always supplemented our in-person, classroom-based courses or simple broadcast-style webinars without substantial interaction. It was exceedingly rare that we'd teach an entire course in a purely virtual environment.

The primary reason was demand. Our clients and their learners did not want virtual instruction because they saw no value in virtual training.

My trainers didn't enjoy delivering virtual training, either. It wasn't fun or fulfilling. The virtual environment didn't offer the same emotional high, that juice you get when you walk into a classroom as an instructor. VILT was uncomfortable for them. They believed, as did our clients, that the only viable way to really teach people was face to face.

We were far more likely to get on an airplane and fly 20 hours to Singapore to deliver a two-day classroom-based course to participants who'd also flown in from various places across the globe than to teach those same students virtually. In those pre-Covid days, the virtual instruction we delivered was mostly on-screen Power-Point slides accompanied with live voice-over. Because of this, we were not particularly proud of our VILTs, so we charged very little for them. That led us and our customers to view virtual training delivery as a low-value option, so we didn't actively pursue the sales of virtual training deliveries.

This was where we found ourselves as we entered the spring of 2020: Asynchronous e-learning was sexy. Synchronous face-to-face training was perceived as the most valuable. And virtual instructor-led training was a low-value afterthought. Then, everything changed.

For 300 years, remote learning had been meandering to shore on a slow-building tide. In 2020, it became a tsunami that washed away the foundational belief that in-person training was the only real way to teach people.

To remain relevant, trainers had to immediately shift the way we were delivering training and engaging learners. Likewise, learners, leaders, and entire organizations had to rethink their negative perceptions of virtual learning. The global coronavirus pandemic moved synchronous virtual instructor-led training into the spotlight and accelerated its broad adoption. VILT finally emerged from the shadows and met its moment.

As March rolled into April, my team at Sales Gravy was catching up fast, scrambling to hold onto our training contracts, retain our customers, and save our company.

The good news is we had two things going for us. First, we had already made significant investments in both technology and developing our competency to deliver high-quality virtual training. Second, our customers, trainers, and learners no longer had a choice. The only way to deliver and attend high-quality, interactive synchronous training was in a virtual classroom.

2

Look Mom, I Built a Virtual Training Studio

In January 2019, I sat down with David Monostori, who leads our creative team, and laid out my plan to build a virtual training studio complex at our corporate headquarters from the ground up.

There were two things driving this plan. First, I was worried about the inevitability of a recession hitting within 18–24 months and that we needed to be prepared. Second, I was very unhappy with the of our virtual training deliveries (see voice-over PowerPoints).

In recessions, travel budgets always get slashed, which is generally devastating to private training companies and corporate learning and development (L&D) departments. However, even in recessions, people need training. In fact, when times are bad, elevating and training talent gives organizations a competitive edge. Back in 2019, my plan had been to prepare to shift to high-quality virtual delivery as a hedge for when the next recession hit.

I also thought we could do better, whether or not there was a recession. Personally, I wasn't proud of our virtual training performance and quality. Our virtual deliveries were often poorly planned and delivered on the fly in airports, hotel rooms, and even cars.

David and I devised a plan to build broadcast-quality sound studios specifically for virtual training delivery. When we presented the idea to the rest of the team, though, it didn't go over well. My CFO was not happy about the massive expense involved in building the studio. The sales and training teams thought we were nuts because, in their minds, no one was going to buy virtual training on a scale that could justify the cost to build studios. To them, I was just another Don Quixote fighting imaginary giants.

We ignored the skepticism and forged forward with construction anyway and built three full-production virtual training studios. A year later, at the beginning of March 2020, the construction crew was still working on the finishing touches and much of the equipment we'd ordered wasn't even out of the boxes. Then, the pandemic stuck. We worked around the clock for several weeks to get the studios ready for action.

This included teaching our trainers to deliver virtual training in a whole new way. Gone forever were the days of voice-over PowerPoint slides. Our trainers stepped out from behind the slides and in front of the camera and we became laser-focused on delivering a legendary virtual training experience. Our new studios gave us the ability to re-create the feel of being in the classroom and interacting with the instructor.

"Our People Won't Accept It!"

With the studios up and running, we were able to beg, plead, and convince our customers to give virtual training a chance. We sent them pictures of our sets, did virtual tours of our studios, and put on our tap-dancing shoes.

Many of our clients pushed back against moving their classes to a virtual classroom. The head of leaning and development (L&D) for a large Fortune 500 client argued emphatically, "Our people won't accept it!" Like so many of our customers, he worried that it would be a low-quality disaster. Such was his experience. Finally, though, we convinced him to give it a try. He agreed, but he forced us to conduct a twice-per-week planning meeting over the three weeks prior to the training.

On that first run, we had people from all over the world in the classroom. Traditionally, these folks would have traveled to the company's headquarters for the training, spending hours on airplanes, days in transit, and thousands of dollars to attend the two-day course that we taught for his company.

Following the virtual experience, we surveyed the participants. They gave the experience a 4.9 on a scale of 5.0. The in-person, classroom experience that we had been delivering for the past three years averaged a 4.7 across all of the previous participant surveys.

This was not what the head of L&D was expecting because, up until that point, his experience with virtual training had been dreadful, and his learners had agreed with that assessment.

One participant commented, "I'll admit, I didn't want to attend this training. But, I'm glad I did. I never thought a virtual training could hold my attention. The training was outstanding." (Most other comments from that session followed this same pattern.)

Our client was convinced—so much so that he hired us to teach his internal trainers to deliver virtual training like ours. It was our very first Virtual Learning Experience® Train the Trainer delivery. Today, his organization is delivering more than half of its courses from a virtual classroom, and the course we teach has remained virtual.

That wasn't a one-off experience, either. In April 2020, we were confronted by a CEO of a mid-sized business-services company that had scheduled a three day in-classroom training with us. He demanded a refund for the course because he didn't want it delivered virtually, which, at that time was our only choice. He hit us with a stream of expletives, among them, "I'm not f@cking doing that [virtual training] to my people."

We managed to convince him to give the virtual training delivery a try with a guarantee that if he and his people didn't like it, we would give him a full refund. As he entered the virtual classroom, along with his skeptical learners, I'll never forget the look on his face as he mouthed *wow* silently. He did not ask for his money back, and we are still delivering virtual training for his company.

Virtual Training Explosion

A couple of weeks later, we were delivering virtual training to a group of sales professionals in India for one of our most valued clients. Because of our history with this company, it hadn't been too difficult to convince them to shift the scheduled physical deliveries to virtual.

Still, there were top executives observing the training because there was so much skepticism (this was true for almost all of our early VILT deliveries). About 10 minutes into the training, we overheard the senior vice president on an unmuted mic calling the CEO and telling him, "Log in now . . . You've never seen anything like this!"

The company subsequently engaged us to deliver virtual trainings to participants in countries all across the globe. We began following the sun from Asia to Europe to North America, teaching people from around the world, from our virtual training studios in Georgia.

Suddenly, at least in the eyes of my team, I went from a man tilting at windmills to a genius. My trainers bought in and my salespeople, for the first time, felt confident selling virtual training. Our clients and their learners loved the experience we were delivering.

Once they experienced our methodology, they were willing to pay a premium for high-quality virtual instructor-led training.

What we hadn't anticipated, though, was that the savings on travel costs and flexibility that VILTs afforded would cause them to double, triple, and even quadruple the trainings they were ordering. In the middle of the worst financial crisis since the Great Depression, our business exploded.

3

The Case for Virtual Training

Before I make the case for virtual training, let's acknowledge that dynamic in-classroom training can be a powerful learning experience. This is especially true when it includes collaborative breakout sessions and experiential learning elements delivered by a talented, passionate instructor. For many participants, perhaps, it provides the very best overall experience on an emotional level. Few rational people would argue otherwise.

The problem is that classroom-based, instructor-led training is both expensive and inefficient. First, there is the investment in the actual training:

- The trainer
- Content licensing (when using a third-party curriculum)

Then there are the expenses for:

- Travel and meals
- Lost productivity while participants are out of the field and in the classroom
- The training space (whether it is a dedicated area in your building, or rented space at a hotel or conference center)
- Printed materials (e.g., name tags, tent cards, handouts, and workbooks)
- Liability insurance
- Indirect environmental costs (e.g., energy consumption, carbon emissions)

More often than not, the investment in the trainer (and licensing, if applicable) is dwarfed by the expenses that aren't directly related to the actual training. We surveyed our clients and found that between 50 and 80 percent of classroom-based, instructor-led training investment is spent on nontraining expenses like travel. With so much money wasted on incidental expenses, in-person training programs make it challenging to get a return on the investment.

These high costs also mean that learning and development (L&D) organizations cannot afford to experiment or make mistakes with physical classroom training. This stifles innovation, agility, and speed when organizations need to change. These incidental costs also put severe limits on the amount of ongoing training that can be delivered by an organization.

The truth is, there will always be a need for in-person classroom instruction for adults. There are some forms of training—for example, how to repair a diesel engine or perform a medical procedure—that require a hands-on learning experience. Yet, even this type of training may be blended and enhanced with e-learning, virtual training, and virtual and augmented reality components to accelerate skill development and mastery.

What about E-learning?

Of course, you can eliminate most of these costs and rapidly deploy training with asynchronous, self-directed e-learning. Just send learners to your learning management system (LMS) and have them advance through a series of videos, online modules, and assessments.

Most large organizations have made significant investments in LMSs and building out e-learning catalogs. Self-directed e-learning is the hottest segment in L&D, and it's projected to grow to $325 billion globally in the near term.[1]

With e-learning, people may consume training content and learn on their own terms anywhere, anytime, on any device. It is a cheap and easy way to train lots of people fast, with little friction. But driving real learning through self-paced e-learning courses has some serious drawbacks, as anyone who's tried it will tell you. The truth is:

- When left on their own, most people abandon the training. Studies indicate that more than 90 percent of online learners never complete their courses.[2]
- E-learning on its own doesn't work well for teaching complex skill sets and competencies.
- People learn better when they collaborate with other people.

Don't get me wrong, there are certain subjects such as compliance and technical how-to instruction in which e-learning excels. Even so, because e-learning leads to a "set it and forget it" mentality, leaders and L&D professionals tend to take a hands-off approach to directing and monitoring e-learning activities. This dilutes the potential return that e-learning offers because either learners abandon the coursework or just go through the motions to check off the requirements so that they look good on reports.

I've observed, on many occasions, competent people fail an end-of-course assessment that should be so easy that a cat could pass it. This happens because they click through the content on the LMS like zombies without paying attention, just to check the boxes.

Most humans need more than a set of videos to truly learn and adopt new skills and behaviors. Albert Bandura's social learning theory posits that people learn best in groups where they have the opportunity to observe, emulate, and practice new skills together.[3]

People wish to communicate, collaborate, and at times commiserate as they stretch through the process of shifting their mindset and acquiring new skills. Humans long for social engagement and the shared community and experience of a classroom cohort.

Simply put, e-learning is missing that social component, so by itself it is not an effective way to develop competency and drive behavior change.

This is exactly why synchronous classroom-based and virtual instructor-led training is, and will continue to be, an important cornerstone of learning and development initiatives.

Enter Virtual Instructor-Led Training

Virtual instructor-led training (VILT) blends the social learning benefits of classroom-based training with the speed, agility, and cost-effectiveness of e-learning—without the wasted expenses associated with the physical classroom.

This means that organizations are able to deliver more high-quality training and rapidly upskill more people, at a much lower cost, which generates a far higher return on the training investment.

The good news is, for a large swath of curricula, VILT, delivered well, is just as effective as classroom training. Furthermore, because a virtual training curriculum can be chunked into shorter training sessions, it is often superior to classroom training when it comes to making learning stick. Numerous academic studies have proven that humans can better retain and apply learned skills when training is delivered in succinct, easy-to-consume chunks.

Richard E. Mayer's segmenting principle describes how chunking breaks complex curricula and courses into concise virtual sessions.[4] For example, eight hours of physical classroom training might be broken into smaller segments (e.g., eight 1-hour sessions, four 2-hour sessions) with time between each session for practice, homework assignments, and blended e-learning content.

Rather than the firehose-in-the-mouth format that physical classroom training typically requires, VILT redesigns the learning path to work the way humans learn best—in short, sequential chunks of information that layer one lesson upon another and present opportunities for repetition and practice.

Learning outcomes improve further when there is time between these chunks of training for participants to practice new skills in the real world, with supportive instructor coaching. These breaks between training sessions provide a faster feedback loop that accelerates the cognitive process of learning. However, this form of on-the-job experiential learning—learning by doing—is impractical with most classroom-based training (see cost and travel constraints).

Compared with traditional classroom training, the combination of chunking and experiential learning in a VILT environment is often a better investment for organizations. When used together, these two strategies improve the probability that training will stick and the desired behavioral changes will be actualized.

While it is certainly more challenging to re-create the social and collaborative environment of the physical classroom in a virtual setting, VILT more than makes up for this shortcoming in other important ways:

- *Agility and flexibility.* Virtual training may be delivered in almost any configuration over any duration.
- *Low risk and rapid iteration.* It is easier to experiment and pilot virtual training initiatives because the risk and cost of failure is low. Likewise, virtual training may be deployed quickly and

continuously improved with little risk to the organization or negative impact on the learners.

- *No walls and few limits.* Learners may access virtual training sessions from almost anywhere. All they need is an internet connection and a connected device.
- *Session review.* Virtual sessions may be recorded and made available for learners to review in the LMS. If a participant misses a session or needs a quick refresher, it is easy to catch up and stay on track.
- *Enhanced and extended communication.* Interactive breakout groups and discussion boards make it easy for participants and instructors to collaborate, get feedback, and communicate both inside and outside of the classroom.
- *Structure and freedom.* VILT provides both the structured, social learning environment that humans require for true behavioral change and freedom from the confines of the physical classroom.

The virtual training structure—a combination of scheduled live training sessions, in-classroom activities and breakout sessions, homework assignments, self-paced learning, and accountability—makes it far superior to e-learning and most classroom-based training.

One more fringe benefit of VILTs: they're green. Most modern organizations are focused on reducing their overall carbon footprint. Similarly, many employees are concerned about climate change and sustainability.

According to an Open University study, virtual training consumes about 87 percent less energy and produces 85 percent fewer CO_2 emissions than classroom-based training.[5] One more reason to love virtual training.

4 | Experience Is Everything

As our virtual training business exploded, many of my peers in our industry segment called to ask (and learn) about how we'd so quickly pivoted from in-classroom training to virtual. After I shared my story about building our virtual training studios, the responses that followed were typically along the lines of:

"Wow, you are way ahead of the curve."

"Your timing was impeccable."

"You are so far ahead of everyone else."

"You really got lucky."

I heard "You got lucky" a lot. Even from my own family. Trust me, in the moment, with so many other training companies taking it on the chin because they were not able to switch to virtual, I felt lucky.

But it wasn't luck. It was the cumulation of years of observation, experimentation, and hard work. A long time ago, we had recognized that virtual instructor-led training was important, and it was a methodology that we would need to master to be competitive in the future. We understood what didn't work, and why people have an aversion to virtual training. We also knew what we didn't like about delivering virtual training.

We were convinced that the biggest obstacle to gaining wider adoption of virtual training was the experience. Too often, VILT felt impersonal, low-energy, two-dimensional, and uncollaborative. For most learners it was about enduring a painfully boring and awful experience rather than engaging in actual learning.

The good news is that it's possible to control most of the things that make virtual training so bad:

- Instructors who are unprepared or not trained to teach effectively in the virtual classroom
- Poor training delivery methods and practices
- Suboptimal virtual training production, including lackluster video, audio, backdrops, and framing
- Media and graphics ill-suited for on-screen viewing
- Failure to adopt and master the technology required to effectively manage a virtual classroom
- Poor instructional design
- Treating virtual training as an afterthought

All of these elements and more are easily resolved, if you have the will and desire to do so. This begins and ends with a focus on the mission.

Five Truths About Virtual Training Adoption

The most frequent concerns that learning and development professionals have about virtual is that clients, internal customers, and learners won't accept it. This was our biggest worry, too, but our experience has taught us five truths:

1. Most people prefer face-to-face training over virtual training—especially if they have had a bad experience with VILT in the past, which many have.
2. If the only option for training is virtual, most customers (the people paying for or ordering training) will begrudgingly accept that option.
3. If the cost (including travel, materials, and lost productivity) of virtual training compared to physical training is similar, most customers will choose classroom-based training.
4. If the cost gap (including travel, materials, and lost productivity) between virtual and physical training is large, most customers will strongly consider and often choose virtual training over classroom-based.
5. When the virtual training experience is outstanding, clients and learners are much more likely to choose VILT over classroom-based training for future deliveries, and they will book more future trainings than they would if they were only considering in-person sessions.

The brutal truth is that the experience matters more than anything. When you make VILT a great experience for your stakeholders (customers and learners), they'll begin to trust it and be open to more.

The one thing you can take to the bank, though, is that they won't accept virtual training if the experience is awful—no matter what the cost. If the choice is between affordable but bad VILT and unaffordable in-person training, customers will choose no training at all.

There are few people who haven't had the pleasure of sitting through agonizing virtual training sessions. Death by voice-over PowerPoint, delivered by a disengaged or clueless instructor, has an especially bitter flavor. I remember watching in dismay as my son endured one of his professors drone on for 20 minutes in a completely monotone voice-over while a single slide with 10 small bullet points filled the screen. The professor's audio was bad, and he never showed his face on video. Not once did he ask a question or engage his students. There wasn't even any movement on the slide. It was excruciating. My son drifted off into an app on his phone. I was livid that I was paying his private university $40,000 a year for this crap, and I fired off a scathing email to the president of his college.

This was exactly why so many of the executives we worked with were dead set against virtual training. It was why our clients' stakeholders believed that the cost for virtual training should be a fraction of what they paid for classroom training.

The reason there has been so much resistance from leaders, trainers, and participants to virtual training is because the experience has been awful. It's not because of the quality of the curriculum or content. It's not because of the talent of the trainer. It's the experience.

What matters most is the way virtual training is delivered and how it makes both the trainer and the participants feel. When the virtual learning experience is emotionally positive:

- Participants are more engaged, readily embrace new competencies, and the training sticks.
- Participants are more likely to show up to class and be open to future virtual training.
- Trainers enjoy their work and gain fulfillment from making an impact.
- Leaders book more virtual training and are willing to pay a premium for it.
- Organizations blend and integrate VILT into learning and development initiatives.

The real secret to gaining widespread acceptance for virtual training is delivering an exceptional virtual learning experience.

5 | The Five Elements of a Legendary Virtual Learning Experience

I acknowledge that human interaction, collaboration, and social learning reach their apex in a dynamic, physical classroom. It's easiest for learners to build an emotional connection—with instructors, with each other, and to the environment—when everyone is physically in the same space. Therefore, to improve the virtual learning experience, our mission and driving focus is creating as close a facsimile to in-classroom training as possible.

First, consider the hallmarks of traditional, old-school virtual training:

- The primary visual focus is on PowerPoint slides and screen shares, heavy on bullet points.
- The teaching modality is voice-over slides. Typically, the trainer reads the slides to the participants.
- The trainer rarely, if ever, shows their face on-screen.

- The participants rarely see each other and avoid being seen as much as possible.
- There is minimal interaction between the learners and the trainer, and amongst the learners.
- Learners rarely interrupt when they have questions or disagreements.
- Because the trainer cannot see the participants, he or she is less likely to stop and ask questions based on a learner's nonverbal expressions—questions that could pull concerns to the surface.
- Audio and video quality (if the trainers dare show their face) is poor.
- There is little on-screen movement or variety to keep learners engaged and visually involved.

Now, consider the elements of a dynamic physical classroom experience:

- The visual focal point is the trainer.
- Slides and visuals are in the background, typically projected on a screen.
- Participants can see the trainer's facial expressions and body language, providing context and additional meaning to words, language, and voice inflection.
- The trainer's movement, in front of the class, walking around, and while interacting with students, keeps learners engaged.
- Learners can see each other and are more likely to form emotional bonds and feel part of a shared experience. Social learning is maximized.
- Participants are more comfortable interrupting and asking questions when they don't understand or disagree.
- The trainer can see the participants' body language and respond to unspoken questions, confusion, or disagreement and pull these issues to the surface for conversation.
- Training delivery is dynamic, fluid, appropriately nonlinear, and interactive.
- Learning is accomplished through breakout sessions, role-plays, interaction, conversation, laughter, and debate.

Designing our new Virtual Learning Experience (VLX) required us to rethink almost everything about how virtual training had been traditionally produced and delivered. Our goal was to bring the most important and engaging aspects of the in-person classroom experience to VLX.

We reimagined the on-screen video experience including: production software, hardware, and processes; video and audio equipment stacks and configuration; virtual training studio design (both professional setups and VLX-certified home studios for our trainers), video conferencing platform integration and mastery, and smoothing out the process of screen sharing, presenting on-screen visuals, and shifting from the main classroom into breakout sessions.

We also focused on the little things, such as getting trainers' faces on-screen and standing up (you would never sit at a desk and deliver training in the classroom); improving trainer eye contact and awareness; getting learners on-screen; creating safe, interactive virtual classroom engagement; running collaborative breakout sessions; and pre-, post-, and inter-class communication.

Finally, we tackled course design, focusing on rethinking visuals and media for on-screen consumption; the chunking, layering, and sequencing of course content; curriculum structure and flexibility; session length consideration; in-class exercises, role-plays, and breakout sessions; inter-class assignments; assessments, trainer-participant communication, and coaching outside the formal classroom; supplemental blended e-learning elements; and leveraging the learning management system (LMS) to enhance and complete the virtual instructor-led training (VILT) experience.

As we experimented, learned, and iterated our process, we landed on the five elements that contribute to a legendary virtual learning experience:

1. Mission and mindset
2. Production
3. Virtual communication skills

4. Design
5. Delivery

We integrated these five elements into our trademarked VLX approach. We redesigned our classroom courses for virtual instruction and honed our virtual training delivery competencies.

Our overriding objective was to create an experience that was so different from the low expectations that most people had for virtual training that it would immediately change perceptions. We wanted people to say *"Wow!"* the moment they entered our virtual classroom and be excited about coming back for more instruction.

Our mission was to create an experience that engaged learners and helped them grow and develop. We succeeded.

VLX Certification

Once we perfected our virtual training processes, the next step was ensuring that the VLX was consistent across all of our deliveries and with all of our trainers.

Consistency matters. The learning experience falls apart if the trainers within an organization are all delivering virtual training at different levels of proficiency and quality.

Therefore, we developed and implemented a standard VLX Studio Equipment and Technology stack, called a Training Tree, and a VLX Trainer Certification. Each of our trainers was required to go through the rigorous certification process in order to continue delivering virtual training. We also added a pay increase incentive once the trainer was certified.

Consistency further improved the quality of our virtual learning deliveries and allowed us to quickly scale up as our clients demanded more and more virtual training. Our clients and their learners loved it. This fresh and innovative approach to virtual training was incredibly close to the in-person experience, and it removed the cost and friction of classroom training (e.g., travel expenses, costs of taking people out of the field, etc.). As a result, many of our clients decided not to go back to the physical classroom.

Let's Get Started

Now that you understand the potential of VILT, you're ready to learn specific techniques for delivering a legendary virtual learning experience. In Parts 2 through 5, I will walk you step-by-step through each of the five elements: mission and mindset, production, virtual communication skills, design, and delivery. My objective is to teach you techniques that turn the virtual classroom into a powerful learning experience, no matter what you teach.

Virtual Training is the most comprehensive and practical resource ever written on virtual training delivery. It will help you master virtual training techniques, engage, and connect with learners in the virtual classroom, and ultimately make virtual training more human. With each new chapter, you'll gain powerful insights and greater confidence in your ability to deliver successful virtual training.

Before diving in, I suggest taking time to reflect on your past experience with virtual training, the state of your current situation, and your goals and aspirations for delivering virtual training in the future.

Notes and Reflections

1. What past experiences with virtual training—good and bad—stand out in your mind?

   _____

   _____

   _____

   _____

2. What do you feel will be the biggest challenges to getting your leaders, learners, customers, or organization to adopt and accept virtual instructor-led training?

_____

_____

_____

_____

_____

3. What are the best opportunities to add VILTs/which courses in your catalog will be easiest to convert to VILT?

_____

_____

_____

_____

_____

4. How do you feel the overall learning experience of the current VILTs you or your organization deliver measure up?

_____

_____

_____

_____

5. What goals do you have for virtual training in the future (for yourself and your organization)?

_____

_____

_____

_____

_____

Notes:

_____

_____

_____

_____

_____

PART II

Mission and Mindset

The way to get through anything mentally painful is to take it a little at a time. The mind can't handle dealing with a massive iceberg of pain in front of it, but it can deal with short nuggets that will come to an end.

—Joe De Sena, founder and CEO of Spartan obstacle races

6

Mission and Mindset for a Legendary Virtual Learning Experience

Let's keep this real. As trainers, we may be stars in the classroom, but the limelight stops there. When the economy dips, we are the first to go. When organizations separate essential and nonessential workers, trainers are almost always on the nonessential list.

Despite our high profile, trainers rarely win trophies or receive accolades for our part in an organization's success. On corporate org charts, we're often invisible. This is our lot in life. Trainers know that our work matters, but to most executives and leaders, we are expendable.

It is also true that our jobs can be repetitive and, at times, boring. We teach the same material, the same way, week in and week out. The only things that change are the participants, and perhaps the city and training room.

Outside of the classroom, we deal with office politics and internal bureaucracy. It can be exhausting. Your passion is practicing your craft and making an impact on earners, instead your time is often consumed with getting over roadblocks and hurdles planted by leaders who second guess you. People who couldn't teach their way out of a paper bag are quick to tell you how to do your job, and, of course, when the people you train go back into their field roles and don't do things perfectly, you get blamed for their failures. (No one ever considers whether they've received any coaching or support from their manager to give the training a chance to stick.)

In this reality, it is easy to feel unappreciated, jaded, and cynical. It's easy to lose your passion and joy for teaching, and forget why you chose this profession in the first place—to help people reach their potential. This is exactly why you must never lose sight of the mission.

Our mission as trainers is to make a positive impact by helping people learn, grow, develop, stretch, and win. This mission fuels the passion, enthusiasm, energy, and joy we feel when delivering training.

Focusing on the mission helps you block out the noise, over-come obstacles, and breeze past adversity. Mission drive pushes you to improve, learn new skills and methodologies, and adapt to new technology so that you can make an even bigger impact on your learners.

Mission Drive

Mission drive is the passion you feel when you make a true con-nection with the mission. It opens you up to new possibilities for making an impact as a trainer. It pushes you to step out of your com-fort zone and do hard things. Mission drive is the key to breaking through the fear of change and building the discipline to master your craft and deliver a legendary virtual learning experience.

Without mission drive, you cannot and will not be an effec-tive instructor and educator. You won't make an impact—and you won't be happy.

You may go through the motions, but the people you teach will see right through your façade. Without mission drive, you'll treat your learners like part of a transaction, and they'll respond in kind. They'll sit there for the required amount of time so you can talk at them for the required amount of time. They'll get a certificate of completion and you'll get paid for your time—and everyone will walk away feeling empty.

You may be able to get away with going through the motions and faking your passion in a physical classroom, but you will not in a virtual classroom. Your enthusiasm, focus, and passion for teaching are under a microscope in the virtual classroom. When you are not fully engaged, there's no hiding it. Learners know when you are not into it, and they check out. In the virtual classroom, without mission drive, you will fail.

Mindset

"I'm so much better in person!"

"I didn't sign up to talk to tiny boxes on a computer."

"I just don't feel comfortable teaching over a Zoom call."

"I'm so nervous in front of the camera."

"I feel so much more in control when I'm in a classroom where I can see everyone and interact."

"I'm absolutely not going to teach virtually. Never. So, forget it. Don't even bother asking!"

"I'm sorry, I just can't do it."

"I hate virtual training! It's not my thing."

Each of these statements came out of a real trainer's mouth when they were asked to deliver training in a virtual classroom. The last one came out of my mouth multiple times.

If you are a talented trainer who thrives in the physical classroom, I'll bet my book royalties that you've thought similar things about virtual training. I had to get over my own hang-ups and self-consciousness and force myself to step into the virtual classroom.

What made me most uncomfortable about virtual training was the lack of validation I felt. In a virtual setting, I didn't get the same type of feedback as in the physical classroom. I walked away from virtual training sessions feeling empty—as if I hadn't made an impact.

For many other trainers, the aversion to virtual training is rooted in fear. I've looked on as otherwise-competent trainers are pushed to emotional extremes when forced to deliver virtual training. They are totally overwhelmed by the software and production equipment. They're petrified of the camera and feel like a fish out of water. Sometimes, they shut down and become paralyzed.

Take a moment to consider your mission as a trainer. See the problem? These aversions to virtual training are not tied to the mission. They have nothing to do with your learners and everything to do with you. To get over your emotional hang-ups, you have to change your mindset. Instead of thinking about what *you want*, think about what *your learners need*. Instead of focusing on what you're most comfortable with, focus on how you can grow.

It's Not about You

The strongest negative feelings about virtual training are rooted in our own insecurities. That's what happens when we make it all about ourselves instead of focusing on our learners. So, I'm going to be blunt with you and tell you the exact same thing I've told my trainers.

I get that virtual training makes you uncomfortable because I've stood in your shoes. I understand that, especially for veteran trainers who are masters of the physical classroom, you don't feel emotionally connected to your students in a virtual environment. I know exactly how that feels.

Learning how to operate complicated software and equipment isn't easy—it makes my brain hurt, too. All you want is to teach and use your God-given talent to make a positive impact. Learning new tech isn't what you signed up for.

I get that the camera makes you feel incredibly self-conscious and insecure. Talking into a camera and being on-screen can unleash deep-rooted fears and be insanely unnerving.

But here's the brutal truth: You have a choice. You can learn to control your fear, anxiety, and insecurity, and master virtual training. Or, you can become irrelevant.

Virtual training is here to stay, and it will become a bigger part of your life. If you refuse to deliver virtual training, you will find yourself unemployed and unemployable. If you lose sight of the mission and don't change your mindset, you will fail to make an impact. Adapt or become extinct. Get the picture?

The Only Three Things You Control

There is no doubt that rising above the emotions that disrupt your confidence in the virtual classroom is a formidable challenge. It's natural to feel intimidated and insecure. It's natural to doubt yourself. It's natural to want to retreat to the physical classroom, where you feel in complete control.

The truth is, there are only three things you can control:

1. Your mindset
2. Your actions
3. Your reactions

That's it—nothing more. You can choose to:

- Rise above your fears and insecurities and try.
- Get over your self-centered need for validation and instead focus on the mission.
- Dust yourself off when you make an embarrassing mistake and try again.

- Learn new technology.
- Change your attitude and self-talk about being on-screen.
- Rise above your emotions and choose your response.

Been There, Done That, Have the T-Shirt

Even though mastering virtual training may seem impossibly difficult, you can do it. I know this because I've had to go through the
same steps of acceptance and transformation.

I've had to get past an anguishing fear of the camera, learn how
to feel confident while delivering virtual training, and figure out
how to *see* in a virtual classroom like I do in a physical classroom.

At the beginning of my virtual training transformation, even
an hour of virtual delivery would leave me mentally exhausted. I'd
feel so anxious beforehand that at times I couldn't sleep at night.
Nothing felt right. And yet, I survived and kept working at it.

Along the way, slowly but surely, I stretched and grew. Virtual
training became easier, energizing, and more natural. I started to
feel good about my work. The feedback from learners, who loved
the experience, was both motivating and validating.

That's why I know you can do it. All it takes is a decision to
shift your mindset to keep the mission in focus. When you change
your mindset, you change the game—you can change the way you
act and react, even when you feel out of your element. The only
thing holding you back is the bullshit story you keep telling yourself about why you can't.

Learning to See in the Virtual Classroom

Professional trainers are virtuosos with people in the classroom.
They are masters at reading other people, responding to nuance,
and using passion and charisma to connect with learners at the
emotional level. They have the ability to intuitively sense the emotions of other people and respond appropriately.

In the classroom, you connect with your learners through perceiving, controlling, managing, and influencing human emotions that are nonconforming and irrational. The feedback you get from your learners helps you know when you are on or off track, and allows you to adjust on the fly.

Making emotional connections in a physical classroom is far easier than in a virtual classroom. You can see the entire picture and quickly flex your communication style to each learner. Relationships with and between learners form much faster. There is less friction, and it is much easier to get into a flow.

When you are standing in a physical classroom, you can see and interpret the *entire* picture. You see not only your learners but also how they interact with their environment and fellow participants. You have the luxury of reading their eyes, the micro-expressions on their face, and the entirety of their body language. You're also able to read the reactions and nonverbal signals as the learners interact with each other. When you are in a physical classroom, it is easier to:

- Make instant connections.
- Know when to speed up and slow down.
- Flex your communication style and pace to each learner.
- Adjust the curriculum and shape it around the unique challenges of the training participants.
- Get hands-on and understand your learners real challenges, issues, and problems.
- Immerse yourself in breakout exercises.
- Communicate clearly and minimize miscommunication.
- Know when what you are presenting is off-base or missing the mark.
- Accurately read learners and develop coaching questions that provoke awareness, in the moment.
- Compare the words that learners say with their nonverbal communication for congruency.
- Keep learners engaged, because it is far less likely that they'll drift into social media, look at their email, or become distracted in the physical classroom.

Rewire Your Brain

If your primary means of training has always been face-to-face, it's natural to fear that you won't be able to communicate effectively, connect with your learners, or make the same impact in a virtual classroom. You fear that virtual training will lower your effectiveness as an instructor.

This fear is not unfounded. The truth is, the most effective way to build relationships and trust, resolve conflict, brainstorm ideas, collaborate, gain consensus, present ideas, and teach is with physical face-to-face interaction. You know this, and I know this, because we are human.

This is why so many trainers feel out of sorts in the virtual classroom. It's as if their sense of sight has been suddenly taken away—and, in reality, it has.

The eyes manage roughly 80 percent of the information and communication you take in. Visual interpretation of the world and people around you consume at least 50 percent of your brain's computing power. In fact, a far larger part of the brain is dedicated to vision than to hearing, taste, touch, and smell combined.[1] In a virtual classroom, though you may see learners on video, it's cloudy, and never as clear as when you are training face-to-face.

When people lose their sight, their brains rewire to improve and enhance both the sense of hearing and touch.[2] Studies indicate that in response to sensory deprivation, "dramatic cross modal neuroplastic changes in the brain" occur.[3] That's the scientific way of saying that your brain can adapt to better fit your environment.

To truly "see" in the virtual classroom, you must go through a similar rewiring of the brain. This is accomplished through practice and repetition and requires time, effort, and pain to make this mindset shift. The good news is that science is on your side. Studies are emerging that indicate that you can rewire your brain to be more perceptive and emotionally responsive in the virtual classroom.

For example, one study showed that you can train your brain to glean insight from body language and micro-expressions though peripheral vision.[4] That's an important skill for trainers, especially when your sight line is pointed toward the camera so that you are making eye contact with learners. The same goes for audible clues. For example, as you become more perceptive of changes in voice tone and inflection, you become nimbler and more responsive to your learners.

The key to rewiring your brain for the virtual classroom is a commitment to getting past insecurity and doing it—again and again. The more you teach in a virtual environment, the less daunting it feels and the more comfortable and intuitive it becomes. Although virtual training is made possible by technology, it is still a uniquely human endeavor. Training and learning are woven into the imperfect fabric of human emotions. That's why it's so important to shift your mindset.

Before you can get comfortable with the technology and overcome your tendency to be camera shy, you need to commit to making a positive impact by helping people learn, grow, develop, stretch, and win. This gives you the resilience to leverage technology to create the highest level of virtual learning experience. This is what separates average trainers from true professionals.

No matter what you teach, for you and your learners, emotions play a crucial role in the outcomes of your virtual learning experiences. And emotions are driven by your mindset. Your commitment to the mission matters. Relationships matter. Interpersonal connections matter. That is why virtual training, through the lens of human emotions, matters.

7 | Emotional Discipline

Nothing causes learners to lean in, buy in, and trust you more than relaxed, assertive confidence (RAC). In the virtual classroom, RAC is your most powerful emotional state.

When you pair relaxed, assertive confidence with a sound curriculum, mastery of virtual training delivery techniques, and production and technology, you are more apt to build emotional connections with your learners and their knowledge is more likely to stick.

When training, you are onstage. Learners are always subconsciously scanning you for clues about your emotional state and trustworthiness. In a virtual classroom, however, people put you under an especially powerful microscope. They observe your facial expressions, body language, the tone and inflection of your voice, and the words you use. They interpret those clues and alter their perception of you based on how your behavior makes them feel. This is called *emotional contagion*.

Emotional contagion[1] is a subconscious response that allows us to pick up on the emotions of other humans without much conscious effort.[2] Like invisible vibrations, emotions are easily transferred from one person to the other when we are together.

We are constantly scanning those around us for clues about their emotional state. We read between the lines, interpret those clues, and alter our approach to people based on our perceptions.

I've spent most of my life around horses. Horses have an innate ability to sense hesitation and fear. They test new riders and take advantage of those riders the moment they sense that the person is afraid or lacks confidence. Horses have a 10-to-1 weight and size advantage over the average person. If the horse doesn't believe that you are in charge, it can and will dump you.

Learners are no different. Your emotions influence their emotions. When you approach virtual training (and horses) with relaxed, assertive confidence, learners respond in kind. They are more willing to trust you, open up, engage, collaborate, and forgive inevitable mistakes and technology glitches. They lean into you and commit to learning.

A Deep Sense of Vulnerability

The truth is that virtual training makes most trainers feel uncomfortable and vulnerable, which is why we prefer the physical classroom. Few of us haven't felt the instant wave of insecurity the moment we look into the lens of our webcam, or, if we make it past that, when a technical issue strikes. Everything in your body and mind screams at you to *run!*

Interacting in a virtual classroom requires you to put it all out there and be vulnerable without the lifeline of immediate feedback you get in a physical classroom. It's emotional risk with no guarantee that your approach will be accepted or appreciated by your learners, who are likely facing their own emotional hang-ups with virtual communication.

In the back of your mind, there is always that little voice warning you that you'll butcher your words, look foolish on camera, come across the wrong way, that people will laugh at you, that you'll blow it, technology will fail you, or that the learners are bored out of their brains and have checked out. In this state, you become nervous, anxious, and insecure.

You begin focusing your attention on what could go wrong rather than what will go right. This makes it far more likely that in your anxious state, you will click the wrong link or hit the wrong button and create a technical malfunction. It also makes it more likely that if something does go wrong, you'll freeze.

You hesitate, become hypercritical, and beat yourself up over small mistakes that no one else notices. Then, in this state of insecurity, you lose your confidence and your audience. When you lack confidence in yourself, learners tend to lack confidence in you.

Vulnerability, according to Dr. Brene Brown, author of the *Power of Vulnerability*, is created in the presence of uncertainty, risk, and emotional exposure.[3] This vulnerability conjures up the deepest and darkest of human fears: *being rejected, ostracized, or criticized, or embarrassing yourself in front of others.*

These fears are painful demotivators, and they're the number-one reason why trainers shun virtual training.

When you know you *need* to do something that you really don't *want* to do—or when you have a bad experience that contradicts your self-image—it generates something called *cognitive dissonance*. It's human nature to get rid of this conflict and do everything we can to make ourselves feel better. This causes some people to double down on what they're comfortable with, while others shut down entirely.

Like so many trainers, you can wish that you didn't have to stand in front of a video camera and teach. You can wish that you could go back to the good old days, back to the physical classroom. You can wish that it was easier. But we already know how that will turn out for you.

Stop wishing it was easier and start working to make yourself better. To be successful in the brave new world that is dominated by virtual platforms and learning technology, you must ditch your wishbone and grow a backbone.

Emotional Self-Control

Let's review the foundational premise of this book: With virtual training, the learning experience matters more than anything else.

Relaxed, assertive confidence allows you to influence the emotions and experience of your learners in a positive way. In the virtual classroom, you must demonstrate RAC even when you feel the opposite. You must rise above the disruptive emotions of fear, worry, doubt, and insecurity, and you need to ditch your egotistical need to always look good and never be seen making mistakes.

Even if you are shaking in your boots, in front of the camera, you must fake it. You must appear relaxed and poised. Like a duck on the water, you appear calm and cool on the outside even though you're paddling frantically just below the surface.

Mastering your emotions begins with your being aware of them. This allows your rational mind to take the helm, make sense of the emotion, rise above it, and choose your behavior and response. Awareness allows you to make an intentional and deliberate choice to monitor, evaluate, and modulate your behavior so that your emotional responses to the people and environment around you are congruent with your intentions and objectives.

Self-awareness and self-control are like muscles. The more you exercise them, the stronger they get. And the best way to exercise them is to face adversity, challenges, and emotional obstacles head on. In other words, practice.

Obstacle Immunity: Growing a Backbone

During World War II, Lawrence Holt, who owned a merchant shipping line in Britain, observed something that launched a movement. His ships were being targeted and torpedoed by German U-boats. Strangely, the survivors of these attacks were more likely to be old sailors than younger, more physically fit men.

This phenomenon led Holt to turn to Kurt Hahn, an educator who, before the war, had been imprisoned by the Nazis for criticizing Hitler. Holt engaged Hahn to help him understand why the younger, stronger, more physically fit members of his crews died at a far higher rate after attacks.

What Holt and Hahn eventually concluded was the difference between the two groups came down to emotional resilience, self-reliance, and inner strength. Even though the younger men possessed superior physical strength and agility, the older, more experienced men had the emotional resilience to endure grueling obstacles that helped them survive.

Holt is famous for saying, "I would rather entrust the lowering of a lifeboat in the mid-Atlantic to a sail-trained octogenarian than to a young sea technician who is completely trained in the modern way but has never been sprayed by saltwater."

The findings led Holt and Hahn to found Outward Bound, an organization that, ever since, has been helping people develop mental strength, confidence, tenacity, perseverance, and resilience by immersing them in harsh conditions. The experience gives people immunity to obstacles.

Joe De Sena's Spartan Races and military training are designed for the very same purpose—to build obstacle immunity. People are pitted against challenging and painful tests of will. Through adversity and suffering, participants learn how to change their mental state and gain control of disruptive emotions.

You build your emotional self-control through repeated use. When you put yourself in a position to experience a perceived obstacle—like talking to a video camera in a virtual classroom—you push through the accompanying emotions again and again.

There are three steps to gaining obstacle immunity and emotional resilience:

1. You must be ready and open to learning and gaining resilience through the crucible of adversity and pain.
2. You must choose to intentionally face your fears and be willing to make and learn from mistakes.
3. You must push through a state of cognitive dissonance in which you cope with the emotional pain of fear and insecurity while fighting the desire to go back to your old comfort zones.

Once you intentionally begin to face your fears and emotionally uncomfortable virtual training situations, you'll learn to disrupt and neutralize the anxiety that comes right before the obstacle. You'll begin rising above your emotions.

The more often you do it, the easier it will become. Soon virtual training will become routine. You'll gain a sense of mastery and confidence. This leads to higher self-esteem, joy, and improved effectiveness in the virtual classroom.

8

Rise Above Your Tech and Video Camera Phobia

Once you've committed to change your mindset, you're ready to tackle the tech stuff. For many trainers, this tends to be the most terrifying mindset shift.

An unstoppable digital tsunami is rolling over learning and development. You have two choices. You can grab your surfboard and ride the wave, or you can sink and drown. It is a binary choice. There is no in-between.

This chapter offers tough love. If you are making excuses that you aren't good with computers or don't get along with technology, it is a career death sentence. You must get out of your comfort zone and become proficient with new technology now, before it is too late.

I get that technology—especially new technology—makes you nervous. I am aware that learning and exploring new technology can make your brain ache. But I'm not going to let you off of the hook. You may be a talented instructor. However, talent will only carry you so far if you fail to embrace digital transformation.

It hurts me when I see one of our people struggling to learn new technology. One of my trainers was almost in tears as she struggled to learn to navigate our new learning management system (LMS). We leverage our LMS to manage and deliver our virtual instructor-led training courses. She said it was causing her so much anxiety that she could barely sleep and begged me to let her go back to the old way of doing things.

I refused and insisted that she put in the time to learn the new platform because I knew the truth. The struggle was all in her head, and if she failed to embrace our new platform, she would have lost her position with our company. It would have been devastating for her and for our team, but the decision to run from technology instead of embracing it is a disqualifier.

I'm going to say this one more time for the people in the back of the room who still aren't tracking. Trainers that are either unwilling or unable to learn new technology, who shun virtual training because it feels too daunting, will be out of a job.

The future belongs to learning and development professionals who embrace technology and weave it seamlessly into their approach to training. These trainers leverage technology to expand their ability to communicate and connect with learners—to better fulfill their mission. Mastering technology makes you more agile, flexible, and employable.

To future-proof your career, practice the three As:

1. *Adopt:* Be an early adopter of new, cutting-edge technology.
2. *Adapt:* Adapt new technology to your unique training approach.
3. *Adept:* Rapidly assimilate technology and practice until you master it.

Mastering technology gives you wings. You'll move faster, be more agile, and make a bigger impact. Adopt an evolve-or-die mindset and find the curiosity and courage to explore and learn new technology.

Rise Above Video Camera Phobia

At the beginning of our Virtual Learning Experience (VLX) Train the Trainer course, we always poll participants about their biggest challenges with virtual training. The top challenge, by a wide margin, is "being uncomfortable on camera."

Much of this video camera phobia stems from the anxiety we feel when we see ourselves on camera. What is reflected back isn't congruent with how we see ourselves. It's similar to how you feel when you hear a recording of your voice. It's weird, uncomfortable, and doesn't sound like you.

As we begin picking apart our perceived flaws, we become self-conscious and disgusted with how we look. This creates even more anxiety and stress, which leads to deep insecurities. In a recent survey, 59 percent of people said they felt less attractive on video than they do in real life, and 48 percent spent more time worrying about how they looked than they spent preparing for the virtual meeting.[1]

This self-conscious fear of appearing on video is real and, more than any other issue, it holds talented trainers back from fully embracing virtual training and delivering powerful virtual learning experiences than any other issue.

At our e-learning production company, Knowledge Studios, we collaborate with commercial and governmental organizations to design and create customized e-learning content. When working with clients, we often interview their leaders on video so we can include that in the coursework. I've watched the most confident, high-powered executives, people who easily command any room they walk into, lose the ability to speak the moment we put a camera in front of them.

I get it, because I've been in that same position and experienced that same fear. It's difficult for people who know me to imagine that I ever felt this way, because these days I'm on video all the time. There are more than 500 videos on my YouTube channel alone (https://youtube.com/salesgravy).

However, there was a time when I was terrified of being on video. I was self-conscious and self-critical, a perfectionist to the point that I would plan, to plan, to plan to shoot videos but never would. Even though I could stand in front of 20,000 people and deliver a keynote, I sounded like a blithering idiot when speaking to the camera. I hated video.

I realized, though, that my fear of the camera was holding me and my entire company back. So, I resolved to make a change. I started with a commitment to myself to shoot one video a day for a month. I'd set my phone up wherever I happened to be and record a video—often in crowded places like airports to force myself to let go of the fear that other people were judging—then make myself post it online.

Soon I began showing my face on webinars rather than hiding behind slides. There were some incredibly embarrassing moments, like the time I delivered a webinar training with over 2,000 people on the call. My webcam was positioned so that people could only see half of my face, from the nose up. I looked like a Muppet. When I learned what I'd done afterward, I was so mortified I thought I'd die. I remember saying that I'd never do it again. But I made myself get back on the horse.

I've shot a ton of bad videos and delivered some really bad training webinars. My early virtual training deliveries were an embarrassment. Bad audio. Bad lighting. Bad framing. But over time, like everything else in life, the more I did it, the better I became. The more I saw myself on video, the more accustomed and objective I became.

Over time, my confidence grew. I developed immunity to my fear of the camera. I learned how to talk to the camera like it was a person standing in front of me. I became comfortable with video equipment and technology. Along the way, the quality of my videos and virtual training delivery improved dramatically.

To deliver a better virtual learning experience—one that's a closer facsimile to the physical classroom—you must first learn to step out from behind the slides and show your face on camera.

If you are uncomfortable with video—even if it flat-out terrifies you—I guarantee that you can learn to master it. I know this to be true because I've watched so many other people do it. There is no button you can push to automatically make it easy, though. You must make the choice to face this obstacle again and again. You must allow yourself to feel embarrassed and make mistakes until the camera becomes your friend.

Step one is recognizing that other people are not viewing you on video the same way you are. They don't care how you look. In fact, they are much more worried about the way they look. Your insecurity about how you look on camera is 100 percent in your head.

Step two is focusing your attention away from the camera and toward your mission: Delivering value to your learners. Rather than worrying about the camera or the technology, focus on your craft as a trainer and leverage that focused energy to rise above your disruptive emotions.

Step three is practice. It took dozens of deliveries until I felt truly comfortable and at home in front of the camera. Mastery, and becoming immune to camera shyness, requires practice. That means repeating the experience over and over.

9 | Good Enough Is Not Good Enough

In my experience, the most important and challenging virtual training mindset shift is internalizing and embracing the mantra: *Good enough is not good enough.*

I've watched my own trainers and those of my clients struggle with this belief system. The problem: It's *easy* to be good enough and difficult to be legendary.

Discipline to always be excellent and do your very best requires sacrifice. In fact, that is exactly what discipline is: sacrificing what you want now (easy) for what you want most—the mission and making a real impact (challenging). Doing the easy things only serves to make you mediocre. It's the hard things that help you grow.

You Are Onstage and Under a Microscope

Far too many instructors treat the virtual training classroom with less respect than they do the physical classroom. Yet, the brutal truth is that you must be better and more prepared in the virtual classroom than you are in a physical classroom.

In both the physical and virtual classrooms, you are always onstage. But in the virtual setting, you are under an intense microscope.

Everything you do and say, inside the limits of your video frame, is being observed and magnified by your learners. Everything—from what you wear, the quality of your visuals, lighting, sound, audio, body language, facial expressions, voice tone and inflection, the words you use, your emotional state, how well you manage the classroom, how you engage your learners, and your mastery of the training content—is being judged. Those judgments are not based on your intentions but, rather, on those of your participants.

You cannot fake it in a virtual classroom and get away with it. You cannot show up unprepared. In the classroom, raw charisma might allow you to get away with mistakes, lack of preparation, or a weak command of the content, but it won't carry you in the virtual classroom. Your learners will see right through it.

No Margin for Error

On many occasions, in the physical classroom I've called a break to deal with equipment issues (usually a laptop reboot, projector issue, or room temperature). In other situations, I've called a break to allow for a reset: conflict between participants or with me; disruptions; a curriculum that needs an adjustment; or the sense that my learners are overwhelmed and need a mental break.

In the physical classroom, if something isn't going well, there is usually enough time and space to flex and fix it. In one situation, for example, I had a client hire me to deliver a training on outbound sales prospecting. We had one brief alignment call prior to the training, and I wrongly assumed that, since the person who hired me had reviewed the curriculum, she understood what I'd be teaching.

About 60 minutes into the full, eight-hour delivery, I noticed that my students seemed confused, and their questions were not congruent with the content I was delivering. So I stopped and said, "Raise your hand if you are responsible for outbound sales prospecting in your role." Not a single hand went up. No wonder they were confused.

So, I took a 15-minute break to meet with the leader who hired me and discuss shifting to a more appropriate curriculum for the learners. We made the adjustment, the participants engaged, and the day was a success.

Had this been a virtual training, though, I would not have had that chance. The training would have been a bust, the leader would have been livid, and it would have been very difficult to recover.

There is no margin for error, little forgiveness for mistakes, and few mulligans in the virtual classroom. Good trainers can often get away with winging it in a physical classroom, but in a virtual setting, winging it is profoundly stupid. Therefore, you must be much more prepared, dialed in, and aligned when delivering virtual training.

Sweat the Small Stuff

With virtual training, you must be uber-disciplined and strive for perfection in everything you do. Every little detail matters. Even if your learners are not consciously aware of it, their brains know when you sweat the small stuff. They respect and value your investment in their learning experience.

With the right mindset for virtual training, you never accept anything less than perfection, even though you will never be perfect. You embrace the truth that complacency leads to mediocrity. The mark of exceptional virtual trainers is that they pride themselves on their deep attention to detail, even when it is painful, because they know that the little things add up and support the learning experience.

The great trainers believe that continuous improvement is the name of the game. They take time to watch their deliveries, pick everything apart, and fine-tune their courses. Because most sessions are easily recorded, you can go back and watch the game film (something that is rarely possible in a physical classroom due to the cost of shooting video).

Likewise, cutting-edge instructors and learning organizations that are committed to delivering a legendary virtual learning experience make regular, ongoing investments to upgrade and add new production equipment, technology, and learning tools to enhance the learning experience. With this critical mindset, they never, ever allow themselves to accept that good enough is good enough.

Before proceeding to the next section, take a moment to reflect on your mission as a trainer and the mindset shifts you'll need to make to fully embrace and master virtual training.

Notes and Reflections

1. Describe your personal mindset and beliefs about virtual training. How do you define "legendary virtual learning experience?"

   _____

   _____

   _____

   _____

2. What mindset shifts do you feel you'll need to make in order to fully embrace and master virtual training delivery? Are there insecurities you need to confront?

   _____

   _____

   _____

   _____

   _____

3. Considering your current virtual training tech stack, where do you feel you need to invest more time to master and become adept at using the technology to deliver a better virtual learning experience?

_____

_____

_____

_____

_____

4. How might you leverage the obstacle immunity process to develop greater confidence with being on camera?

_____

_____

_____

_____

5. List some of the small things you can do right now to elevate your virtual training game and immediately improve the learning experience.

_____

_____

_____

_____

Notes:

_____

_____

_____

_____

PART III

Production

If you compromise what you're trying to do a little bit, you'll end up compromising a little more the next day or the next week, and when you lift your head you're suddenly really far away from where you're trying to go.

—Spike Jonze, director and producer

10 | The Brain on Virtual Training

Take a moment to imagine if TV shows and movies looked like most virtual training sessions. You'd be instantly turned off by the poor production quality. You certainly wouldn't want to pay for it or come back for more.

Traditionally, the phrase *virtual training production* has been an oxymoron. Little value was placed on production quality to make the on-screen visual experience equivalent to what we expect to see on a TV screen. Trainers just spin up Webex, Adobe Connect, Go-To-Meeting, Teams, or Zoom, throw up some slides, and start talking—from wherever they happen to be. This is a key reason why the virtual learning experience has been so awful for learners.

When watching a video, your brain attempts to interpret the picture it sees on the screen and compare it to what it expects things to look like in real life. When the picture on the screen does not look natural, the brain must work harder to fill in the gaps.

This increases the viewer's cognitive load,[1] meaning the amount of work the brain has to do, to fill in the gaps. This requires the brain to exert extra energy and computing power to scan the patterns on the screen in an attempt to make sense of them.

If we were to take an MRI scan of your brain during a typical video call, it would appear stressed and overheated. This is exactly why even 30 minutes on a video call can leave you feeling exhausted.[2] Most video calls, by their nature, are poorly produced. So many things are out of place: out-of-sync audio, lighting that makes people look unnatural, poor framing, and virtual background dysfunction are just a few. (We'll talk about all of these issues in the rest of Part Three.) And as these elements pile up, we feel what has been labeled *Zoom fatigue*.[3]

Now let's contrast that with the feelings we get when watching movies and TV shows. We don't get "Netflix fatigue" or leave a movie theater feeling utterly exhausted. We binge shows because those shows make us—and our brains—feel good. An MRI scan of your brain while streaming your favorite shows would reveal that your brain is cool, relaxed, and happy.

Much like a computer, the human brain can process only so much information at one time. As the cognitive load grows, the brain slows down and becomes less efficient. It is unable to focus.

From a purely evolutionary standpoint, cognitive overload can lead to catastrophe. When your brain gets overloaded, it cannot focus. This could lead to missing a threat that puts you in danger of being removed from the gene pool. Think texting and driving.

For self-preservation, as cognitive load increases, the brain begins to tune out anything it deems boring or unimportant, in order to remain focused on potential threats.

What trainers and L&D organizations too often fail to grasp is that poor virtual training production is actually painful to learners' brains and can impede knowledge acquisition and actualization.[4]

Poor-quality production in virtual training increases the cognitive load on your learners' brains. Attention control diminishes, both short- and long-term memory are negatively impacted, and it becomes more difficult for learners to connect with you and focus. When your mission is to make knowledge stick to effect competency development and behavior change, this is a very bad thing.

Step into the Video Frame

Before we dive deeper into a discussion of virtual training production, I want you stop for just a moment and visualize a physical classroom setting. In this classroom, there's an aisle down the middle and four rows of tables on each side, four chairs to a table. You, a participant, are sitting in the first row.

In front of the room is a projector and a screen. The instructor's laptop is connected to the projector. A PowerPoint slide is being projected onto the screen.

You can hear the instructor's voice reading the bullet points on each slide. But you can't see her face because she is standing behind the screen. You can only see her legs from the knees down.

Every once in a while, she stops before clicking to the next slide, and asks, "Does anyone have any questions about this?" No one ever answers, leaving only awkward silence. So, she clears her throat and moves on to the next slide and begins reading the next set of bullet points. She never steps out from behind the screen.

Sound ridiculous? It is. This wouldn't happen in a physical classroom. You would never throw your slides up on the screen and then stand behind it while teaching. That would be asinine, and there is a good chance your learners would get up and walk out.

In a physical classroom, you stand in front of the class. You, not your slides, are the center of attention. You, not your slides, drive the training and create a dynamic, interactive learning space.

This is exactly how you should teach in a virtual classroom. Your face should be on video most of the time, with your visuals and on-screen media in a supporting role. You need to be the star.

In Part Two, we discussed how the camera can cause fear and insecurity. Some readers may experience a wave of anxiety just reading this section. Still, I must be straightforward and blunt. *In the modern virtual classroom, you may no longer hide behind your slides.* Just like when you are training in a physical classroom, you need to step out in front of your slides and graphics and into the video frame, to engage and interact with your learners.

The days of voice-over PowerPoint virtual training are over. That training modality is boring and tired. Rather than engaging learners, it turns them off and exhausts them. It is a terrible experience, and the only reason trainers punish their poor learners with this old-school delivery method is their own self-centered fear of the camera.

The good news is that most people have become comfortable interacting with family and friends via video. Likewise, we've grown accustomed to jumping on video calls for meetings with our colleagues and clients.

However, as you likely know, a video call to your mom or a meeting with your peers is far different than conducting virtual training on video. In the virtual classroom, the stakes are much higher. You are always on stage. Participants are observing everything they see in your video frame, including:

- Your appearance
- Facial expressions and body language
- Lighting and audio
- Video quality and clarity
- Your backdrop and training set
- Your position in the video frame

They use this information to make conscious and subconscious decisions about whether they like you and trust you, and whether they will fully engage in learning.[5]

Humans feel first and think later. In other words, it is all about the experience. Emotion is a huge driver of experience and, like Zoom fatigue and cognitive overload, it tends to happen on a subconscious level. For this reason, it is incumbent on you to get over your hang-ups with the camera and master virtual training production.

Triggering the Negativity Bias

It's human nature to focus more on what is wrong than what is right, and anything that is wrong sticks out like a sore thumb. This *negativity bias* causes your learners to ask, "What's wrong with this picture?" instead of looking for what is right. Much of this happens at the subconscious level.

Learners are scrutinizing you inside your video frame. You are on stage, and every behavior and word is being observed. Your audience looks for congruence between your words, nonverbal communication, and actions, and uses this information to decide whether to trust you.

Poor production exacerbates the negativity bias. For example, if your lighting is bad and learners can't see your facial expressions as you explain something, it's much more difficult for them to connect the dots. They're going to question your credibility, at least on a subconscious, emotional level. Even if they consciously cut you some slack, it's hard for them to get past their feelings that "something just doesn't feel right."

As a trainer, you must never discount the power of the subconscious mind. It holds sway over learners' perceptions, emotions, behavior, interpersonal interactions, likes, dislikes, and conscious decision to embrace the training and learn.

The trap many trainers fall into is the false belief that good intentions and mastery of the curriculum are enough. They show up for virtual training believing that the content of the training is all that matters, forgetting about the perceptions they are creating within their video frame.

Think about it. Would you walk into a big interview wearing a T-shirt, shorts, and flip-flops? Of course not, because no matter how talented you are or how good your resume, credentials, and references—no matter how well placed your intentions are—the image of you dressed that way would create such a deep negative perception that you would not be offered the job or welcomed back.

Learners are not judging your competency as a trainer based on *your* rational intentions. They make those judgments based on their emotional perceptions. If people already have negative perceptions of virtual training, their subconscious mind magnifies anything in the video frame that supports those beliefs. This is called *confirmation bias*, which is a fancy way of saying that people see what they are expecting.

While they aren't aware of it, their preconceived ideas lead them to say to themselves, "I knew this was going to suck!" This is why you must work to neutralize any of your learners' negative subconscious biases that are likely to generate poor experiences in virtual training.

If you are committed to delivering a legendary virtual learning experience, begin with improving production.

Ramping Up Virtual Training Production to Create Wow! Moments

One of my favorite things about good virtual training production is hearing learners say, "*Wow!* I wasn't expecting this." I enjoy watching their faces light up the first time they see our production quality. More than anything, I love the comments that our virtual learning experience completely changed their perception of virtual training.

Poor production quality is one of the three big reasons that virtual training gets such a bad rap. The other two are poor virtual training design and delivery, which we'll address in upcoming chapters. Investing to improve these important elements is 90 percent of the virtual training game.

At its foundation, virtual training is essentially a live-streamed, interactive, educational TV show with you as the host/facilitator, and it should be treated that way. It is a production, and all related aspects of a good show matter: lights, cameras and camera angles, audio, set, graphics, wardrobe, and switching. Never forget that virtual training is both education and entertainment.

We consume a massive amount of broadcast and online video at an ever-accelerating pace: TV, movies, YouTube, Facebook, Instagram, TikTok, and a growing list of streaming services, including Netflix, Amazon Prime, Disney+, and many more. Video accounts for 75 percent of internet traffic and is projected to rise to 82 percent in the near future.[6] There is more video content being produced than you can watch in your lifetime—even if you were sitting on your couch 24 hours a day.

Because we have so many choices, and the competition for viewers and attention is so fierce, the overall quality of video production—even from amateurs—has improved dramatically. Along the way, we've grown to expect a certain level of excellence. This expectation extends to the virtual classroom. In the age of streaming, learners are no longer willing to endure poor-quality virtual training production.

Instructors, along with learning and development organizations, must up their game. Never allow yourself the excuse, for one moment, that your training content and curriculum can carry the day on its own. It can't, and it won't! The moment you enter this mindset, you make the choice to degrade the learning experience and reduce the probability that knowledge will stick and behaviors will change. Instead, you must commit to providing the best possible visual experience for your learners.

High-quality, live-streamed production was once cutting edge. Now, it's an essential element of the virtual learning experience. Production is how we make the virtual classroom a closer facsimile of the physical classroom and a training modality that captures the hearts and minds of learners.

11 | The Essentials of Highly Effective Virtual Training Production

The directors and producers of TV shows and movies invest hundreds of hours into perfecting their sets, lighting, and audio. On the major shoots I've been on with professional crews, twice as much time was spent on getting the cameras, lighting, audio, and set right as was spent actually shooting the video.

Professionals make this investment of time because they know that viewers know what looks right and wrong, even if they are unaware of it at the conscious level. Directors and producers are acutely aware that the more natural things look to the viewer's brain, the lower the cognitive load and the easier and more enjoyable the content is to consume.

This is your primary goal with virtual training. Just like producers and directors, you need to invest time to create an on-screen experience that makes you look natural on camera and as close as possible to how you might look if you were teaching in a physical classroom.

It takes effort to get it right. You need to care about the details and approach things with a focus on your audience. You must be intentional about optimizing every aspect of your virtual training set.

Videoconferencing technology is good and getting better. Professional-level video equipment continues to become less expensive and easier to use. Today, you can build a decent virtual training set for less than a thousand dollars. For around a few thousand dollars, you can build an impressive professional-level set that will raise your virtual training game to new heights.

Later in this section, I'll walk you through advanced virtual training production and our Virtual Learning Experience (VLX) Professional Studio set-up. Before we dive into the advanced equipment, let's explore the essentials and basics that you will need for virtual training production.

Because technology and equipment are always evolving, I am not going to provide specific equipment recommendations within these pages.

Instead, we keep an updated list with links to recommended equipment for your virtual training set, along with other resources to help you up your virtual training game, at https://www.salesgravy.com/vt. With the purchase of this book, you get free access to the Virtual Training resources for 90 days. Just use code: VTB2021X when you check out. No credit card or payment of any kind is required.

Audio

Film studios invest in massively expensive sound stages because audio quality is critical. This is why, in many cases, audio technicians get paid more than camera operators. Audio is that important.

Likewise, with virtual training production, the most important element is audio. High-quality audio matters. If people can see you but cannot hear you, your training session will be a failure. If your audio quality is poor, it creates a bad impression and makes for a challenging learning environment.

There are also studies that demonstrate how poor audio on live-streamed video is a key culprit of increased cognitive load, fatigue, and mistrust.[1] This is why, with virtual training production (and all video production), audio comes first.

The Four Keys to Good Audio Production

There are four elements to consider for professional-level audio quality: internet connection, background noise, room echo, and microphone quality. The good news is that you have a lot of control over these, and the following tips will set you on the right path.

Ensuring Good Internet Connection and Speed

Your internet connection has a great deal of impact on the quality of your audio. If the connection is poor, there will be times when your voice cycles in and out or becomes distorted—no matter how good a microphone you have. One way to address this is to upgrade your internet plan to the fastest speed your provider offers.

If your connection or speed is poor or inconsistent, dial in with your phone. That way, no matter what happens to the image on screen, training participants will be able to hear you—even if the overall audio quality streaming on the platform is poor.

Eliminating Background Noise

Do not run virtual training in rooms or spaces where background noise is an issue. Trains, traffic, alarms, doorbells, pets, other people talking, and random loud noises affect your audience's experience and *your* ability to maintain attention control.

Eliminating background noise is so important that we spent tens of thousands of dollars treating our virtual training studios for sound. We built double walls with an air pocket in between, clad the outside with a sound barrier, and installed special sound-blocking insulation in the walls just to keep outside noise from penetrating into our studio.

We've also installed *on-air* and *quiet* lights outside of our studios and in the common areas of our office to alert our team to keep the noise down.

I highly recommend that training organizations make similar investments and build virtual training studios inside offices and training centers. The investment is well worth it over the long haul.

What if you don't have the means to build a sound studio? If you deliver virtual training from home or in a regular office, there are certainly ways that you can reduce background noise without spending big bucks. For example:

- Ensure that pets are locked out of the room.
- Put a notice on your door or outside of your training space to alert others that you are in session.
- Disconnect your doorbell or put a note on it asking people not to ring it.
- Turn all devices on silent and ensure that there are no appliances, plumbing, electronics, or other systems on that might create noise in your training space.
- Place sound blankets in front of window and doors susceptible to environmental noise.
- Move your training set away from outside walls and windows susceptible to environmental noise.
- Schedule deliveries and interruptions for times and days when you are not training.

Avoiding Room Echo

Few things are more irritating than audio that echoes off the walls. When your voice is echoing, people have a hard time hearing you and paying attention. In movies and on TV, you rarely hear dialogue that has an echo because it makes the experience terrible.

Most offices and rooms in your home have walls made of sheetrock. Sound bounces off of it like a rubber ball off of concrete. If your room is sparsely furnished or has high ceilings, it will be even worse. You will sound like you are in a cave.

The best way to test your room is to make a recording speaking into your normal microphone. Then listen. If there's an echo, fix it. Begin by finding another space with better sound. If that is not an option, there are a couple of actions you can take:

- Start by adding more soft furniture to your space. This will absorb some of the sound and reduce the echo.
- Treat the room with sound blankets, acoustic panels, rugs, and corner bass traps. It is critically important that you place sound absorbing material in front of you (behind your microphone).

Ensuring Microphone Quality

As you deliver training, you want your voice to sound natural, full, and clear, so it's as close to being in person as possible. Your voice should stand out and cause learners to lean in.

If you listen to most people on video calls, their voice sounds compressed and tinny. This is because they're either using a cheap headset microphone or the microphone on their laptop.

I am not a fan of wearing headphones or headsets of any kind. It creates a poor visual. Even though the person on the other side of the video call knows why you are wearing them, the reason does not compute in their subconscious brain. We are used to staying at arm's distance from people wearing headphones. Headphones or wireless earbuds send a clear message: "Do not bother me." You wouldn't wear headphones during a physical training, and you should not wear them in a virtual classroom.

Start with a good-quality external microphone. In many cases, a podcast or shotgun microphone can be placed out of the scene so things on-screen look natural. Rode and Blue are our favorite brands of podcast or shotgun microphones. For lavalier microphones, Rode and Sennheiser are our favorite brands.

My personal preference is a high-end lavalier mic. It delivers superior audio quality, allows me to move around freely on set, keeps my volume constant and consistent, making things feel more natural, as if I am there face to face.

Lavalier microphones have a receiver and transmitter, plus a small microphone on the end of a wire that fits into the transmitter. The quality of the small microphone can make or break your sound. The best microphones make your voice sound clear, help dampen room noise, and reduce the negative impact of echo.

Some high-quality external webcams have built-in microphones. Though the sound quality isn't as good as a professional mic, it's better than your laptop mic and most earphones.

Finally, in a pinch, some of the new wireless earbuds like Apple AirPods Pro have far better audio quality than the microphone in your laptop.

Most of our trainers pair a lavalier microphone with a professional-quality podcast mic as a backup. On days when one virtual training delivery runs into another, having a backup mic saves the day when the lavalier mic batteries die.

You'll find resources for treating your training space for sound along with links to our favorite microphone options here: https://www.salesgravy.com/vt Remember to use code **VTB2021X** when you check out to gain free access to these resources.

Lighting

Next to audio, lighting is the most important technical element of a video sales call. Just like your eyes, cameras require the right amount of light to render a good image.

Great lighting makes you look natural and accessible, and it reduces participant brain strain. It also illuminates your facial expressions, making you appear more human and trustworthy. For those of us who are a little vain and worry about how we look, nothing will improve your image on camera more than quality lighting.

The good news is that it is relatively easy to get lighting right on your virtual training set. The first step is to eliminate bright light sources behind you (like windows). Webcams and cameras may automatically adjust to and record the brightest source of light in the frame. When that light is behind you, you're no longer in focus and your face appears as a dark blob on-screen. We call this frame *witness protection*.

If you are in a room with a window, face the window. Natural light helps accentuate skin tone and features; however, if it is too bright or there are harsh glares, it can be distracting and wash you out. Manage and regulate natural light sources with shades or sheer window treatments. Be sure to check and regulate bright light sources on each side of your face that may cause washout or create unflattering shadows.

For the best lighting, use either LED ring lights or LED panel lights made specifically for shooting video. Make sure that the lights you choose have a dimmer and temperature control so that you can adjust the brightness to achieve the most natural look.

For a basic studio, use two or three lights placed on light stands. The light stands allow for adjustments to the height and angle so that you eliminate shadows and get the perfect lighting angle. You'll want the light source to be roughly the same level as the camera and directly behind it. Don't place your lights above you because it can create distracting shadows that may distort how you appear on camera.

In our professional sound studios at Sales Gravy, we mount lighting from the ceilings and use floor and hair lighting to remove shadows and create contrast. We invest a great deal of time ensuring the lighting is at the right temperature, reducing glare, eliminating shadows, and calibrating lighting with our camera settings and lens.

You'll find recommendations and options for lighting in the free book resources here: https://www.salesgravy. com/vt.

Cameras and Lenses

There are three types of cameras to consider for virtual training production:

1. The built-in webcam on your laptop or desktop computer
2. An external webcam with a built-in lens, such as a Logitech
3. A professional mirrorless camera with a separate lens

Choosing the right camera setup can make a huge difference in the quality of your video frame and how you appear on-screen.

Let's begin with a cardinal rule for virtual training production: *Do not use your computer's built-in camera!* These cameras produce a low-quality image. They also cause framing issues.

For example, using your laptop's internal webcam can turn you into the *Grim Reacher.* You'll notice this look when a person is using their webcam on video calls and reaches for the keyboard. Suddenly their hands become massively large compared to their head. It is not a flattering look (more on this later).

For the best quality, choose a camera that is external from your laptop and place it on a sturdy, adjustable tripod. There are excellent, high-quality webcam options available that will make you look professional without breaking the bank.

Take it up a level with a professional mirrorless, full-frame camera (we like Sony cameras) paired with a high-quality, wide-angle lens. This setup requires a capture card or professional switcher. You'll find several recommendations and options for cameras, along with information on setting up mirrorless cameras using a capture card, in the free book resources here: https://www.salesgravy.com/vt.

Internet Connection

No internet connection, no virtual training. Poor internet connection, poor virtual training session. It is that simple.

I mentioned this in the section on audio, but it bears repeating: Spend the money to upgrade to the fastest *upload* speed your broadband provider offers. Most providers tout their download speeds. That's great for streaming movies, but doesn't help a bit with delivering a video training livestream. For this, you need to max out your upload speeds.

Most importantly, avoid connecting to the internet via wi-fi during your virtual training sessions. Wi-fi is unreliable and often unstable. There are many, many reasons why your wi-fi signal may lose strength—just consider how many devices and things in your office or home are connected to wi-fi. Any of these devices and a host of other issues can wreak havoc on your signal strength and degrade your virtual training quality.

Instead, connect directly to your router with an ethernet cable. An ethernet cable (and an adapter dongle, if your computer does not have an ethernet port) is the least expensive component of your virtual production set and will have the greatest overall long-term impact on the quality of your on-screen presence and peace of mind.

Like many people, you may live or work someplace where speed and bandwidth go up and down, depending on the day, weather, node, or how many people are on at the same time. For this reason, I highly recommend investing in a backup connection source like a mobile hotspot. Having a backup source has saved me on many occasions when my main broadband source was weak or went down.

We've included a tool to check your internet speed here: https://www.salesgravy.com/vt.

Video Conferencing Platform

Your video conferencing platform is the virtual classroom. It is where and how you and your learners will meet.

We are big fans of Zoom. In my opinion, it is the best platform for dynamic, interactive virtual training. The learning experience is unequaled. As I write this book, many of the other platforms are doing their best to catch up to Zoom's breadth of features and ease of use. Zoom is setting the pace. More innovative platforms will emerge as video conferencing, virtual events, and virtual training continue to become an ever-integrated part of our lives.

Your company, organization, or client may dictate which platform you use to deliver your virtual training. As a private training company, at Sales Gravy, we must be competent with every platform, including Zoom, Adobe Connect, BlueJeans, WebEx, Teams, and Go-To-Meeting, among others. Our trainers and producers are comfortable working with all of them.

To be effective for virtual training delivery, your platform should be secure and support:

- Ease of use and access for learners
- Breakout groups
- Spotlighting (choosing which frames are on-screen) and gallery view options
- Chat, polls, and questions
- Recurring meetings
- Screenshare features
- Session recording options
- *Bonus: virtual whiteboard*
- *Bonus: direct integration into your learning management system (LMS)*

The most important action you can take as a trainer is to invest time into exploring the features of your platform and taking the tutorials.

You need to know your platform intimately, inside and out. Be a student of it. Know the shortcuts. Become an expert so that you can quickly troubleshoot issues and help other people who may have trouble connecting or navigating. No excuses. Know it and master it.

 We've included links to platform tutorials at https://salesgravy.com/vt. Remember to use code VTB2021X when you check out to gain free access to these resources.

12 | Virtual Training Backdrop

What learners see when they enter your virtual classroom sends a powerful message. Your backdrop is essentially everything that is visible in your video frame other than you. Your backdrop should be both functional and visually appealing.

Let's begin with backdrops that are never acceptable for virtual training delivery:

- Clutter and trash
- Unflattering and inappropriate personal items that distract learners
- Plain blank walls—especially white or beige
- Distracting paintings and art
- Anything that could potentially be considered offensive
- Bright windows
- Big, cavernous rooms (like your family room) that have a tendency to pull learners' eyes away from you and into the room

You should also stay away from using the background image replacement feature on your videoconferencing platform. Though the technology is getting better, it has severe limitations for delivering dynamic virtual training.

Background replacement works best when you are sitting still. Fast movements and hand gestures can cause blurs and break the artificial background, making you look distorted and unnatural. This is why *background replacement doesn't play well with virtual training.* Because you'll often be standing up, using hand gestures, and moving around while you deliver training, phony backgrounds create a poor visual experience for your learners.

Elements of an Effective Virtual Training Background

Let's go back to the physical classroom. As a participant, what do you see?

Typically, there will be a screen or monitor on which slides are projected and a whiteboard or flip chart that allows the trainer to record participant responses and supplement with illustrations while teaching.

Replicating this scene is one of the ways that we make virtual training closer to physical training.

- Our trainers stand up during sessions, just as they would in a physical classroom.
- Behind them on one side is a monitor mounted on a stand, on which we project slides, just like in a physical classroom.
- On the other side is a whiteboard or flip chart used to capture ideas and supplement the slides, just like in a physical classroom. In some of our studios we have installed smart boards that double as a monitor for projecting slides and a whiteboard.
- Behind the monitor and whiteboard, the backdrop is a branded fabric display (like what you might see at a press conference).

The stretched fabric backdrop eliminates any potential distractions, supports our brand, and always looks professional. Most of these displays are portable, making it easy to relocate the virtual training set.

Alternatives to the fabric backdrop include bookcases, textured walls such as brick or stone, or your actual corporate training room. We love our brick and stone backdrops. Participants always comment on how good they look.

A well-crafted, built-in bookcase neatly filled with books and a limited number of tasteful knick-knacks that support your personal brand can also be a good backdrop. This backdrop offers enough variety to be interesting but not distracting. You can take a look at some of our professional backdrops in Figures 12.1 through 12.3.

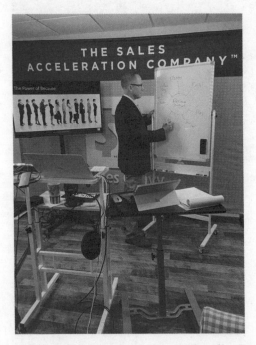

Figure 12.1 Trainer Home Studio Backdrop

Figure 12.2   Sound Studio Backdrop

Figure 12.3   Textured Backdrop

The key is that your backdrop be professional, send the right message to learners, and create the closest facsimile to physical training as possible.

Monitors

A flatscreen monitor on which slides are projected in the background is an important part of your set. It a visual reminder to participants that they are in a classroom, and it keeps slides visible while you are on-screen, engaging participants.

We use a switcher to toggle the slides on and off screen (inside the video frame) during the training production. We'll discuss switching in greater detail in Chapter 13.

For your monitor, choose a flat-screen TV with a matte finish. This will help knock down the glare from your lighting. Mount it on a mobile stand so you can easily adjust its position and further reduce glare.

Smart Boards

In a few of our studios we have installed smart boards that serve as both the monitor for projecting slides and the whiteboard (Figure 12.4). The smart board is expensive, but it really enhances the virtual classroom.

Prior to class, our instructors add graphics and documents that support the session lesson plan to the smart board. From the board, they are able to access the internet and files from cloud storage.

During class, all participants have access to view and (when allowed) edit the whiteboard in real time on their own devices. We also use it during breakout sessions. Each group has its own page on the board. Instructors can see their discussion notes in real time, just like in a physical classroom. The smart board facilitates

Figure 12.4   Smartboard

powerful collaborative conversations and is a game changer for virtual breakout sessions.

The board doubles as the monitor and allows the instructor to write on and annotate the slides during discussions and instructions. A full PDF of all the content captured on the whiteboard is given to participants following the virtual session—something that is rarely possible in a physical classroom with normal flip charts.

We've included resources for building a professional virtual training backdrop, monitors, whiteboards, and smart boards in the free book resources here: https://www.sales-gravy.com/vt. Remember to use code VTB2021X when you check out to gain free access to these resources.

13 | Live Switching

The top two complaints from participants about virtual training are:

1. They hate awkward pauses and uncomfortable silence.
2. They don't feel engaged in the learning process. In other words, they feel like instructors, on poor-quality virtual training sets, just talk at them.

Resolving the first complaint is where live switching comes into play. (We'll address the second complaint later.)

Think Like a Television Producer

You are accustomed to experiencing live switching when you watch reality shows and sports on TV, but you probably take it for granted. TV always looks that way, so you hardly notice it.

To understand live switching, think about watching a live sporting event on television. What you experience on-screen is a mix of wide-angle shots, close-ups, reaction shots, overhead angles, and split screens. The point of view is constantly in motion. Yet the switches are fluid transitions—so smooth that you don't think about them. You just know that it looks and feels right.

This is what we expect. Without live switching, the event would be dull, boring, and lack the on-screen action that grabs our attention and pulls us in. The on-screen motion and camera switches break patterns, keep our brains engaged, and discourage us from tuning out.

For exactly the same reasons, switching is just as important during virtual training deliveries, which are essentially interactive live TV shows. In fact, this is why you should start thinking like a television producer and director. *"OK, Camera one, hold your position. Camera two, begin slowly zooming in on Coach Clary. OK, let's cut to camera two for the reaction shot now. Switch to camera three on my mark—four, three, two, go . . ."*

Whether you are switching between multiple camera angles, as we do in our virtual training studios, or just between your camera and slides, you should be thinking the same way. Mastering switching is one of the keys to delivering a legendary learning experience.

Show Your Face

Before we move forward let's review a point that I made earlier. Voice-over PowerPoint is dead!

You, not your slides, should be the star of the show.

The brutal truth is that if you delivered your training with no slides at all, but your face was on-screen the entire time, your learners would have a better experience than if you had incredible slides, but they never saw your face.

During our *Virtual Learning Experience Train-the-Trainer Bootcamps*, we run drills in which trainers are forced to run sessions with no slides. The participants in the audience are always shocked at how much better the deliveries feel when the trainer is on the screen most or all of the time.

This does not mean that visuals are not important. They are. We use visuals extensively in our training sessions. But the visuals do not and should not dominate the screen.

Our trainers are the focus. With the magic of switching, we deliver a powerful on-screen experience with frictionless toggles between:

- The trainer on full screen
- Slides on full screen
- A picture-in-picture frame with the trainer appearing in a box over the slide
- Trainer writing on the whiteboard/smart board
- Smart board on full screen
- Participants engaging with the trainer on full screen
- Breakout sessions
- Role-play sessions with the players spotlighted, side by side on the full screen
- Different camera angles for effect and variety

Showing your face on-screen makes your training more personal and memorable, and it keeps learners more engaged. It's much easier for learners to check out when the only thing on-screen are slides. When you are on-screen, you gain credibility and build trust because when learners are able to see you, they are more likely to believe you.

Four Ways to Switch

Back to the mission and objective. Your mission is to make a positive impact on the people you train and help them learn, grow, develop, stretch, and win. You will achieve your mission more effectively through virtual training, when you also achieve your objective of making virtual training as close as possible to physical classroom training.

At its foundation, live switching is about making virtual training sessions smooth and seamless, so they amplify the production quality. It's about elevating the on-screen experience so that the participants lean in, engage, learn, and ask for more. It is how we achieve a physical classroom feel in a virtual environment.

The video sources on a virtual training set are what send images to the video frame. These can be actual cameras, a screenshare from your computer, another device running visuals, a TV monitor, or a smart board.

For example, in Studio Green, which is my favorite training studio at Sales Gravy, we have five actual cameras, an Apple TV unit that runs my slides from an iPad, and the output from the smart board. Everything feeds into a switcher and, from there, we decide which source to display in our videoconferencing software.

Of course, this is an example of a complex production that requires the services of a professional producer. There are four ways, from basic to complex, to switch your video sources. No matter what your situation, however, to truly master virtual training delivery, you must also master switching.

Self-Produced on a videoconferencing Platform

The most basic way to switch is to manually toggle between full screen video, screen share, and breakouts using just the features of your videoconferencing platform.

This is exactly how most trainers have traditionally managed switching from their camera, to slides, to screen shares.

This is also why there are so many complaints about awkward pauses and uncomfortable silence. If you have ever done manual switching like this, and I bet you have, you already know how challenging it is. There are so many moving parts, and it takes time to find and make the switches.

If manual, self-produced switching is your only option, then it will be absolutely critical that you practice using your platform shortcuts until you can make switching as smooth as possible.

You must prepare in advance, getting everything you intend to share on your desktop ready to go (and keep everything else out of sight). You'll also need to either plan and set up breakout groups in advance or randomize them so you can move to breakouts with one click.

When you are hunting and pecking to find the right file on your cluttered desktop or the correct button to click on your platform, it is mind numbing platform, it is mind numbing for your learners.

Producer on Platform

A better way to switch using only the features on your video-conferencing platform is to have another person produce your training.

Your producer will manage what appears in the main spotlight frame, switching between you and your slides, managing and switching to breakout groups (giving you much more flexibility), and spotlighting learners during role-play.

In this scenario, you'll want to run your slides on another device that is logged into the meeting. Your producer will simply toggle between spotlighting your video and the slides on the other device, eliminating awkward screen share.

Self-Produced with Professional Switching Device

The most effective way to do live switching when you are self-producing (running your own show) is with a professional mini video switcher (see Figure 13.1). Using a professional switcher will help you deliver an elevated virtual learning experience.

A video switcher is a device that allows you to decide which video feed you want to send to the platform with the push of a

Figure 13.1   ATEM Mini Switcher

button. It also allows you to manage your microphone, use the picture-in-picture effect, and choose other effects and transitions like wipes, dissolves, and fades. It's like holding a miniature TV studio in your hand.

Most switchers that are appropriate for self-producing allow you to attach up to four video sources. The core function is allowing you to easily and smoothly switch between sources with the push of a button. Because it is so easy, you don't even need to look at the switcher to change sources, which creates a fantastic effect for your learners.

With self-produced virtual training, you'll typically have only two sources attached to your switcher via HDMI.

The switcher will connect directly to a computer that is logged into your video conferencing platform. You will select it as your video and audio input (when running audio through your camera or the switcher) on the platform.

The first source is your main camera. For best results, use a professional mirrorless camera connected directly to the switcher. Be sure to have your microphone running through that camera so the main video and audio feed are together.

The second source will be your slides and visuals (I suggest embedding any videos into your slides for easy playback). Your visuals will need to be housed on a separate device from the one that is logged into your videoconferencing platform. You will connect it to the switcher via an HDMI cable.

On our sets, we use iPads to run visuals. The iPad is connected to an Apple TV via Air Play. The Apple TV connects to the monitor or smart board behind the trainer and the monitor connects into the switcher. This is just one configuration, and it works exceptionally well—especially for playing video. When the Apple TV is connected to the smart board, we are able to toggle between the smart board and slides (Figure 13.2).

Optionally, you can connect other camera sources or devices. For example, you may want a close-up camera pointed toward your whiteboard. In my case, I like to use a separate camera angle when I am inside breakout rooms to create a different look and feel that is closer to how I might engage a breakout group in a physical classroom setting.

Here is an example of a simple switching cadence in which you toggle between visuals and your face on-screen with just two simple button pushes:

- When you move to a new slide, put it up on-screen.
- After you've made your point on the slide or series of slides, switch back to your face on the full screen as you ask questions and engage with learners.

Figure 13.2   Connections to ATEM Mini

- When you are going to remain on a slide for more than 90 seconds or there are multiple points to cover, switch to picture in picture mode so that learners can see your face while you present and during the discussion.
- As you pause to interact, get feedback, ask and answer questions, review breakout results, demonstrate, or role-play, switch to your face on full screen.

We are big fans of Blackmagic switchers and use them in all of our studios. You'll find links to our favorite switchers in the free book resources here (use code **VTB2021X** to get free access): https://salesgravy.com/vt.

Produced with a Professional Switcher

The most advanced virtual training production is achieved with an onsite professional producer using a broadcast quality production board (Figure 13.3).

The producer runs everything—switcher and platform—so that the trainer can remain completely focused on the participants. In some cases, with complex training scenarios, multiple camera

Figure 13.3 Professional Production

angles, and live green-screen keying, we'll add a director to guide the trainer as we make camera angle switches.

It is virtually impossible to run a complex, multicamera production without a producer in the booth. This is out of the reach of most individual trainers working from a home or office set. However, training organizations that wish to deliver exceptional virtual learning experiences should consider this level of production.

The key, when working with a producer, is developing and reviewing a run of show. This will include a review of the session curriculum, slides and transitions, breakouts, exercises, role-plays, and multimedia.

For example, prior to virtual training sessions, I provide my producer with a list of participant names and assigned breakout groups, discuss the timing for cycling me in and out of breakouts, and plan when I will shift to different camera angles and when to use picture-in-picture or live key my visuals onto our large green screen.

The goal, in all four switching scenarios is a smooth training delivery, devoid of awkward pauses and uncomfortable silence, that is as close to physical training as possible. Think like a television producer.

ABOUT SALES GRAVY STUDIOS

We built our sound studios from the ground up for the primary purpose of producing high-quality, world-class virtual training and e-learning content.

We have invested thousands of hours and hundreds of thousands of dollars in building a world-class production facility and processes to go along with it.

For organizations and leaders that want to build in-house studios, our team can help you move faster and avoid costly mistakes. We offer hands-on consulting to help you build and equip your virtual training studios, do it faster, and at a lower cost.

To learn more about how we can help you, visit https://salesgravy.com or give us a call at 1-844-447-3737.

Reflection

Before proceeding to the next section, take a moment to reflect on your current virtual training set and equipment. Consider how you might improve the learning experience, working with the equipment you already have and making adjustments to your setup. Make a note of the investments you'll need to make to elevate your game and deliver a legendary virtual learning experience.

1. Go back and watch a few of your virtual training deliveries through the eyes of a learner. How would you rate the production quality?

   _____
   _____
   _____
   _____
   _____

2. What are some immediate actions that you can take to boost the production quality of your virtual training deliveries? Set both short-term and long-term goals.

   _____
   _____
   _____
   _____

3. Make a list of your current virtual training equipment. Consider what you'll need to acquire or add to the mix to take your virtual training set to the next level.

   _____
   _____
   _____
   _____
   _____

4. What adjustments do you feel you'll need to make to your current training set to improve lighting and audio quality?

5. What do you feel are the biggest obstacles to elevating your virtual training production quality, and how might you overcome those obstacles?

Notes:

PART IV

Virtual Communication Skills

The physical world is similar to the virtual world in many cases. It's about being aware.

—Amy Jo Martin, entrepreneur and author

14 | Be Video Ready

In the virtual classroom, you are on stage. Your physical appearance is a key element to making a great impression, along with projecting credibility and competence.

A recent study from Princeton University concludes that people judge your competence based on what you wear and how you look. People who are well-groomed are deemed more competent.[1] "These judgments are made in a matter of milliseconds and are very hard to avoid."[2] Therefore, you need to look your best. Always on. *Always video ready.*

Grooming

On video, good grooming is essential. The camera is unforgiving, and poor grooming sticks out like a sore thumb. Your hair, face, teeth, and makeup are being scrutinized by stakeholders, and you are being judged based on what they see. And once someone makes that split-second decision, the negativity bias is hard to overcome.

For women and men with long hair, style it back away from your face. This will prevent it from casting unflattering shadows and keep you from touching and fidgeting with it. No matter what length your hair is, make sure it is styled and neat. A little hair gel or paste can go a long way toward making you look phenomenal.

Gentlemen with facial hair should keep it trimmed neatly. Unkempt facial hair looks extremely unflattering on camera.

Makeup can make everyone look healthier on camera, and moisturizer can give you a healthy and nourished look. For women, a normal makeup routine should be enough. A little blush on your cheeks can add dimension so the bright lights don't wash you out. Men should consider wearing a little bit of concealer to even out dark under-eye circles and cover up imperfections and blemishes. It is also a good idea to brush on a very light coat of translucent powder, made specifically for video production, to reduce shine.

Video platforms like Zoom have a touch-up feature that can make you look younger and smoother. It adds a blur effect, and it works! However, it should not be used on your training set because it may also blur anything behind you, like a whiteboard, monitor, or smart board. You don't want to do anything that will make it difficult for your learners to see.

Wardrobe

Just because you are delivering virtually rather than face-to-face does not mean that you can relax your discipline to dress professionally. In fact, virtual training raises another set of considerations.

Before getting into the details, here are my two rules for your virtual training wardrobe.

> **Rule number one:** You must dress at the same level you would if you were walking into a virtual classroom. In most cases, this means conservative business casual. If you wouldn't wear it in a physical classroom, then don't wear it in a virtual classroom.
>
> **Rule number two:** You must dress for the camera. It is important to consider how what you wear will look in the video frame on-screen.

Wardrobe choices to avoid:

- Avoid black, which can negatively impact lighting and accentuate unflattering shadows and dark circles under your eyes.
- Avoid pastels and very bright colors like white, neon, or vibrant reds.
- Avoid white or pastel shirts unless they are covered with a vest, sweater, or other garment that minimizes the reflection from such light colors.
- Avoid colors that clash with your backdrop or match its color.
- Avoid shiny fabrics.
- Avoid patterns. On camera, patterns can create a weird strobe effect called moiré.[3]
- Avoid garments with too much drape and fold. These types of outfits cause shadows and are not flattering on camera.
- Avoid garments that are stained or wrinkled. Even virtually, people will be able to tell.

Wardrobe choices that work:

- Choose colors that look best on camera like blues, greens, deep reds, and pinks. I'm a big fan of blue, especially light-blue shirts. Blue pops on livestream video and is very flattering.
- Choose a shirt with a collar. Collars are professional and send the message that you mean business. I almost always wear a suit or sports jacket on camera.

- Choose clothes that are properly fitted and flatter your build and body shape. Be sure they fit well and do not bunch or ride up.
- Choose clothes that are comfortable and breathable. It can get hot under the lights.

Accessories

Choose conservative and understated accessories. These items should support your outfit without becoming the center of attention. You should avoid wearing any large accessories that reflect light, that make noise, dangle, or move. If you wear glasses, be sure they have a nonreflective coating (or adjust lighting angles to reduce glare).

I recently sat through a video presentation with a presenter who was wearing a bracelet that make a loud sound each time to she put her arm on her desk. It was such an irritating noise—like fingernails on a chalkboard—that I was unable to concentrate on anything else. By the end of the meeting, I wanted to run away as fast as I could. I can't even remember what the presentation was about.

Enclothed Cognition

Beth Maynard, Sales Gravy's Vice President of Curriculum Development and a senior master trainer, was amused when my son asked her why she was wearing high heels during a virtual training delivery. Her response was, "This is what I wear in a physical classroom, and I dress for success in the virtual classroom. My shoes make me feel confident."

There is a reason why our customers and their learners love Beth. She is the consummate professional. Her criticism of a lot of virtual training wardrobes has stuck with me. She says that far too many trainers approach their on-camera looks like the infamous mullet hairstyle: business on the top, pajamas on the bottom.

Which begs the question: *Should you wear pants and decent shoes when you are delivering training in a virtual classroom?* There are two reasons why the answer is an emphatic *yes!*

First, your brain knows when you are not wearing a complete, structured outfit. This impacts the way you think and your mood, attitude, and behavior. Your clothes have an effect on your psychological processes, including emotions, self-esteem, and inter-personal interactions. Scientists call this *enclothed cognition*.[4]

When you dress your best, you feel your best. You have more emotional control, are more relaxed, and feel more confident. For most presentations, you will be standing (see Chapter 16); comfortable, professional shoes that enhance your posture will only improve your confidence. Wearing a complete, polished outfit puts you in the frame of mind for teaching.

Second, you don't want to get caught with your pants down. Embarrassingly, this happened to an ABC news reporter who was doing a segment from home. "Camera framing and digital graphics made it appear as though he was fully dressed in the beginning of the segment. But toward the end, his bare legs began to show on-screen," wrote Hannah Yasharoff in a column for *USA Today*.[5] Suddenly, millions of people were left to wonder whether or not he was wearing shorts or only his underwear. For reporter Will Reeve, it was "hilariously mortifying."

We'll chalk up Reeve's situation to unintentional wardrobe malfunction, but trust me, you don't want this to happen to you. A wardrobe malfunction on live TV during the 2004 Super Bowl halftime show almost cost Janet Jackson her career.[6]

So, lose the sweatpants, shorts, and pajamas. Put your pants on. Complete your outfit. Dress like the professional you are.

15 | Video Framing

At least half of human brain capacity is dedicated to the eyes and sight. The primary way we interpret the world around us is through visual stimulus. This is exactly why your face, rather than slides, needs to be in the video frame most often during virtual training sessions.

When learners can see you in the frame, the experience feels more natural and human. They may observe your facial expressions and body language, and pick up on emotional nuance—information that adds texture and meaning to the information you are teaching. When you are in the frame, human-to-human connections form quicker.

But it is not good enough to just be in the frame. Framing is about how you present yourself to your learners. Your frame must put you in the best light and reduce cognitive load so that it is easier for participants to focus and learn. You already know how much production quality matters, and video framing is a key component of high-quality virtual training production.

Remember that the objective is to deliver an experience that is as close to in-person training as possible. Therefore, the you that learners observe in the video frame must look natural and position you in the most positive manner.

Framing is where everything you learned about lighting and cameras in Chapter 11 gets put into action. It is a combination of the right equipment, your set, camera angles, and positioning. Proper framing makes you look professional and confident. It pulls learners in and grabs their attention, reducing fatigue and increasing engagement.

The bad news is that many trainers make egregious, self-inflicted errors with framing. The good news is that these errors are easily corrected with just a little bit of intentional focus.

Six Frames That Cause Negative Perceptions of You

Remember our conversation in Chapter 10 about cognitive load? You'll recall how cognitive load increases when things don't look right in the video frame and the brain must work overtime to fill in the gaps. High cognitive load causes fatigue, degrades memory, and makes learners tune out.

Your position within the video frame has a massive impact on your learners' cognitive load and how they perceive you as a trainer. It determines whether you look natural, as if you are right there in front of your participants, or distorted in a way that leads to brain stress.

There are six video framing positions that negatively impact your appearance and increase cognitive load (Figure 15.1). We gave these poor framing positions names to make them easier to identify and correct.

SKYDIVER   BOBBLEHEAD

STARGAZER   WITNESS PROTECTION

MAX HEADROOM   GRIM REACHER

Figure 15.1   Poor Video Frames

Skydiver

This is the most common framing mistake. In this position, the trainer is looking down into the camera. In extreme cases, you can even see the skydiver's ceiling.

This is not a flattering position as it has a tendency to accentuate dark circles under your eyes and create a double chin effect.

It also sends the unintended message that you are talking down to your learners.

This tends to happen when the trainer uses the webcam on a laptop computer that is positioned lower than their face (e.g., on a desk, table, or lap). This means the trainer's line of sight is above the camera.

Witness Protection

This is the second most common framing mistake. In this position, the trainer has a bright light directly behind them, typically, a window filled with sunlight. Because the camera will focus on the most intense light in the frame, the trainer's face becomes obscured and dark on the screen—like you might see in an interview with someone in witness protection. In extreme cases, with very bright lights, the trainer appears completely blacked out.

This framing mistake makes it difficult, if not impossible, for learners to read your body language and facial expressions. It is the most stressful frame position for the brain to perceive, and it causes an exponential increase on your learners' cognitive load.

Bobblehead

In this position, the trainer is too close to the camera. Their head, from the neck up, fills the entire frame. In extreme cases, parts of their head and face are completely cut off. Because learners are unable to observe body language and hand gestures, it becomes more difficult for them to interpret meaning and draw congruence from your words.

This position may also trigger a low-level flight-or-fight response in learners. Imagine how you might feel if someone was that close to your face in person. You'd likely feel a wave of anxiety and back up to get away. This type of emotional response degrades short-term memory, which negatively impacts your learners' retention of what you are teaching.

Max Headroom

In this positioning mistake, there is too much space between the top of the trainer's head and the top of the video frame. With severe headroom issues, your head appears teeny tiny at the bottom of the frame (we call this look Mini-Me).

This framing position is typically caused when you adjust your laptop in an attempt to resolve the unflattering double chin effect caused by the skydiving position. If you overcorrect, the camera will be angled above your head.

Stargazer

This framing position is similar to the Max Headroom problem. In this mistake, the trainer's laptop is positioned too high, causing them to look up into the camera. This makes their face appear weirdly distorted.

Grim Reacher

The Grim Reacher effect occurs when the trainer reaches toward their keyboard to share their screen, chat, or manage the video conferencing platform. As they reach in, their hands become huge and distorted. It is as if someone stuck their hands right into your face—instantly revolting.

Proper Framing

The most common cause of poor framing positions result from using your laptop's webcam. Too often, a laptop camera is too high, too low, or too close. Wherever your laptop is positioned, your camera is positioned, which is extremely limiting. Therefore, the first step of proper framing is to STOP using the internal camera on your laptop or desktop computer—*now!*

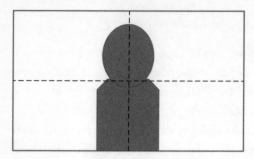

Figure 15.2   Proper Framing

The best way to visualize proper framing is to think about how a newscaster is positioned on-screen. If you take a moment to turn on your favorite news show, you'll notice that when the newscaster is in the frame, the horizontal and vertical axes line up with the room. The horizontal axis for the frame is parallel to the floor and ceiling, and it's perpendicular to the vertical axis, which is parallel to the walls (Figure 15.2). It's like the frame is a perfect slice of the room, straight up and down. The camera is straight (not tilted, as with the Skydiver and Stargazer positions).

You should be positioned in the center of the frame with your sight line at camera level. This ensures your eye contact is the same as if you were teaching in person. Ensure that there is reasonable space between the top of your head and the top of the frame, but not too much so that you make the Max Headroom mistake.

The easiest way to resolve framing mistakes is to use an external camera—a webcam or professional mirrorless camera—mounted on a tripod behind your laptop that can be adjusted to eye level. If you absolutely must use your laptop, place it on an adjustable laptop stand so that the camera is at eye level.

You should be far enough away from the camera that your torso is visible above the waist. This ensures that your face is not so close that it looks distorted, as in the Bobblehead position. It also keeps your hands visible when you speak, just as you would be in the physical classroom.

16 | Body Language

Decoding and Encoding Nonverbal Communication

When you observe other people's body language and interpret it for meaning, it's called *decoding* or deep listening (we'll discuss this in Chapter 22). When you are sending cues to other people—like your learners—it is called *encoding*.

A distinguished list of researchers have done extensive work on the impact of nonverbal cues on human communication. More than half of human communication is nonverbal.

For example, a study by Dr. Albert Mehrabian found that, depending on the situation, our actual words account for 7 percent of what people are decoding. The other 93 percent of what we communicate comes from our tone of voice (38 percent) and body language (55 percent).[1] According to Mehrabian, body language and tone of voice are especially important when they don't seem to reflect the speaker's words (noncongruence).

What this tells us is that our nonverbal signals have a massive impact on our ability to connect with and influence other people. This is why encoding is a meta-skill in the virtual classroom. When you're training virtually, your nonverbal communication is being put under a microscope and scrutinized by learners for meaning, so you must be disciplined with managing what learners see in your video frame.

The Three Elements of Body Language

Learners are listening to the words you *say* and comparing them to your body language for alignment. To be an effective, approachable, trustworthy communicator in the virtual classroom, there are three elements of body language that you must control:

1. Facial expressions
2. Gestures and movement
3. Posture

When these elements are not congruent with the words you are saying, learners begin to question your credibility and believability. This is exactly why proper framing is so important.

Facial Expressions

Reams of research conducted over the past fifty years tell us that we can truly read a face like a book. Your face is expressive. It reveals what you are feeling, whether it's happiness, concern, fear, anger, or surprise.

When we are interacting with other humans in person, we are constantly scanning their faces in an attempt to judge their emotions. This same process is in play in the virtual classroom. On video, though, it is much harder to read facial expressions.

This is especially true when your video frame suffers from poor lighting (as with *witness protection* framing) and positioning. When you are in dim lighting, standing too close to or far from the camera, your learners have difficulty discerning your micro-expressions[2] and emotional nuances. It is because of these challenges that you must ensure that you have a good camera, lighting, and proper framing.

Your learners are going to look at your facial expressions to decipher meaning and make decisions about how they should be responding and even feeling, based on what they see. To be successful at encoding, you must ensure that you don't miscommunicate your intentions, or that learners misjudge your facial expressions.

Since learners can only see what is in your video frame, they do not have the same reference points that are present in a physical classroom. Inside this limited picture, their brains are hard at work filling in missing pieces. Therefore, your facial expressions take on even greater importance. You must be more intentional about controlling your expressions than you would be in person.

For example, consider your resting facial expressions. This is your normal expression when you are listening to someone or concentrating. Often when I'm reading, thinking, or writing, my wife will ask me if I'm mad. It surprises me that my facial expression leads her to make assumptions about my mood that are often the opposite of what I'm actually feeling.

What she is responding to is my RBF (resting bitch face) or RAF (resting asshole face), as she likes to call it. Most people have some form of this resting facial expression, which confuses other people. It can be a big miscommunication problem in the virtual classroom, especially when you are observing a breakout session, fielding questions, or running role-plays.

Victor Borge is credited with saying, "The shortest distance between two people is a smile." From the moment we are born, we learn that smiling is the fastest way to get others to pay attention to us. A baby's smile lights up the room. Smiles attract. Even dogs understand this. A wagging tail, an upturned mouth, and bright, wide eyes are the fastest route to a pat or treat.

Smiling is a primary communication tool used to connect and bind us to others. Numerous scientific and psychological studies have shown that the smile is a universal language that is recognized across cultures and ethnicities around the globe.[3] Excitement, humor, pleasure, confidence, happiness, welcome, love, understanding, caring, kindness, and friendship are all communicated through the smile.

In your video frame, a bright, pleasant smile is the most powerful and effective facial expression. Period. A smile makes you instantly likeable. It's welcoming. A sincere smile humanizes you and conveys authenticity. It sets learners at ease and creates a relaxed environment.

Your sincere smile says, "I mean no harm. I'm open." In this more relaxed state, you will find that training participants are more likely to engage, more willing to answer your questions, more forgiving of mistakes, and emotional connections develop faster.

Smiling is encoding at the highest level. From the moment the virtual training session begins and until it ends, I am intentional about smiling and being more expressive. Because people respond in kind, learners tend to smile back at me. When your facial expressions make your participants feel relaxed, they will naturally become more engaged in learning.

Gestures and Movement

We talk with our hands.[4] People watch our hand gestures and use those signals to connect the dots between facial expressions, voice inflection, tone, and words. Generally, we use our hands while we are speaking without thinking and people interpret the meaning of our gestures subconsciously.

Hands are a big part of body language. Making your hands visible on-screen is important because, to trust you, learners need to see that your words and body language are congruent.

When learners can't see your gestures, your behavior may be misinterpreted as stiff, cold, aloof, or uninterested.[5] This is exactly why you should stand up while delivering training in the virtual classroom, framed from the waist up.

Other types of body movement are also important to consider. On-screen movement keeps learners' brains activated and tuned in. You might lean in when something is important, move back when you want to reduce the intensity or set people at ease, and move side to side when you wish to make a point. It goes without saying, but the only way to incorporate this type of movement is to stand up, which brings us to my next point.

Posture

Rule number one on our virtual training sets is that trainers stand up. This is not optional and it's not a suggestion. We stand up in the physical classroom and we stand up in the virtual classroom. When you stand up, you instantly project passion, energy, confidence, and become a more effective trainer.

Consider the perceptions and judgments that learners might make about you based solely on your posture, stance, and body movements. How you position yourself in the frame and move on camera sends clear nonverbal messages.

If you take an objective look at trainers who sit rather than stand during virtual deliveries, you'll notice a number of poor behaviors that create a negative impression:

- Poor framing positions = causes learners to check out
- Leaning in too close to the camera = face distortion
- Slumped or hunched over = low energy and insecure
- Leaning back in the chair = disinterested, not enthusiastic

- Fidgeting in the chair, back and forth or side to side = insecure, untrustworthy, distracting

None of these positions make you look confident, competent, or passionate about the subject you are teaching. Yet when you are sitting at your desk, these positions are all too easy to assume. Because you sit at your desk all day, they've become habitual—making these posture and positioning mistakes almost impossible to break.

This is exactly why we stand up when delivering virtual training. Standing is a core element to delivering a legendary virtual learning experience. When you stand up, you transfer confidence, passion, and enthusiasm to your learners. You grab their attention, and they are more likely to engage.

Standing up also makes it much easier to keep the sightline between your eyes and the camera level, and you'll naturally be framed better in the shot. It also allows you to create movement on the screen just like when you are training in person.

Research by Amy Cuddy of Harvard University demonstrates that "power posing," physically standing in a posture of confidence, causes you to feel more confident.[6]

Standing up not only elicits a change in emotions,[7] but it also triggers a neurophysiological response, which releases the hormones cortisol and testosterone, and these play a significant role in creating the feeling of confidence.[8]

When you feel and act confident, you are more credible and believable, which gives your learners more confidence in you.

17 | Eye Contact

It is always easier to communicate when we can see each other eye-to-eye. Our eyes connect us at an emotional level like nothing else. The eyes really are the windows to the soul.[1] When I want to know how my wife is feeling, I don't ask. I look at her eyes. They tell me everything.

The eyes and the micro-expressions around the eyes are how we gauge a person's mood, truthfulness, and approachability. Consequently, in our effort to make virtual training as close a facsimile to physical training as possible, we must be intentional about making eye contact. This means looking directly into the camera.

On video, learners cannot see the entire picture, which can them make them feel uneasy. Thanks to the negativity bias, they are much more likely to assume the worst when they feel that you are not making eye contact.[2] They may think that you are:

- Insecure and lack confidence
- Hiding something
- Disinterested and detached
- Not paying attention
- Not listening
- Uncaring

Maintaining regular eye contact is one of the most challenging aspects of virtual training. It is much easier to make and maintain eye contact in person than it is on video.

One of the big reasons why maintaining eye contact on video calls is so difficult is that instead of looking into the camera, we tend to look at ourselves. Studies and surveys indicate that most people spend 30–70 percent of the time on videoconferencing platforms looking at their own face.

According to a survey conducted by Steelcase, 72 percent of people get distracted by their own appearance on video.[3] Why are we so distracted? Because we believe we look horrible on video.

When you are on camera, it is very difficult not to look at yourself because you know that people are looking you. We stare at the gargoyle we see on-screen and pick apart everything about ourselves until we are utterly disgusted.[4] This can be nerve wracking, causing deep insecurity and a negative impact on your confidence and self-esteem.

Of course, during an in-person training, if you spent half the time looking at yourself in a mirror, you'd likely feel the same way. But you would never do that. If you stared at yourself in a mirror while teaching in a classroom, your learners would eventually walk out on you.

For this same reason, you need to break the habit of looking at your own video frame during virtual training deliveries and develop the habit of looking into the camera.

1. Start by making a commitment to stop looking at yourself.
2. Then, either hide or minimize your video frame and maximize your learners' frames.
3. Finally, practice looking into the camera while you deliver training until it feels natural.

The Eye-Contact Paradox

Developing the habit of looking into the camera instead of the screen requires massive effort. The Steelcase survey also found when people were not looking at themselves on-screen, they were looking at the other people on their screen. Thus, breaking eye contact.

This is the great eye-contact paradox:

- When you look directly into the camera, the learners feel that you are making eye contact. This is a very good thing.
- However, when you are looking into the camera, it does not feel like they are making eye contact with you.
- This causes you to feel uncomfortable and disconnected. Emotionally, you long for their eye contact and the feedback it gives you while you are training.
- In this state, you look away from the camera and at their frames on your screen in an attempt to make eye contact (and feel more comfortable).
- As soon as you shift your line of sight away from the camera, it causes your learners to feel that you have broken eye contact with them.

Since you are the trainer, it is your responsibility to make eye contact and build an emotional connection. Despite your discomfort, you must have faith that when you are making eye contact with the camera, you are connecting with your learners. When you learners feel connected they will be more comfortable and engaged in your virtual classroom.[5]

The good news is that standing with your torso visible in the frame creates more distance between you and the camera. With this increased distance, you gain a wider view of the screen making it easier to see the faces of your participants while maintaining eye contact.

There are a few things you can do to make this work even better. You can set your computer on an adjustable stand so that it is just below your camera, or you can place a large screen behind your camera. In both of these arrangements, you'll be able to see your learners in your peripheral vision. This will give you enough of a view that you can glean insight from their body language without breaking eye contact. It takes practice, but with repetition you can absolutely train your brain to do it.[6]

We build our virtual training sets with monitors a couple of feet behind the camera to make it easier to look into the camera and see our learners at the same time. This allows our trainers to "look through" the camera and at their participants. Everything is positioned to help us maintain the proper line of sight (Figure 17.1).

From time to time, you may need to look away from the camera to read your notes, find a resource, or even deal with people who stick their heads into your training set and interrupt you. When this happens, never forget that your learners cannot see the entire picture.

The moment you look away, their brains attempt to fill in the gap. Because of the negativity bias, they assume the worst. The easiest and most effective way to neutralize this bias is to simply

Figure 17.1 Sightline Camera Monitor Setup.

pre-frame what you are doing. Saying, "I need to look away for a moment to find something in my notes," is all it takes.

Some of our sets have huge monitors behind the camera. When we do training in these environments, we do some pre-framing at the beginning of the virtual training session. As I'm going over the agenda, for example, I'll gesture outward and say, "I have a massive screen in front of me on which I can see each of you. I've set my screen to gallery view so that I can see everyone. If you notice me looking away from the camera and at another part of my screen while we are having a discussion, it's because I'm looking at you."

Once they know why I'm breaking eye contact and it makes sense to them, their negativity bias is neutralized. It works like a charm.

You can learn more about our monitor-behind-the-camera setups in the free book resources here: https://salesgravy.com/vt. Remember to use code VTB2021X when you check out to gain free access to these resources.

Reflection

Before proceeding to the next section, take a moment to reflect on your own challenges with communication in the virtual classroom and changes you can make to deliver a better virtual learning experience.

1. How might you elevate your wardrobe selection to make a better impression on-screen?

   _____
   _____
   _____
   _____
   _____

2. On your next video conference call, choose gallery view and have fun identifying the six framing mistakes.

   _____
   _____
   _____
   _____
   _____

3. Go back and watch a few of your virtual training deliveries. Take a moment to identify framing mistakes you may be making and consider adjustments you should make before your next delivery.

   _____
   _____
   _____
   _____
   _____

4. As you watch replays of your virtual training deliveries, focus on your body language and consider adjustments you might make to ensure there is congruence in your message.

   _____
   _____
   _____
   _____

5. Practice standing up and making direct eye contact with the camera.

_____

_____

_____

_____

_____

Notes:

_____

_____

_____

_____

_____

PART V

Design and Delivery

Good teaching is one-fourth preparation and three-fourths pure theatre.

—Gail Godwin

18 | Essentials of VILT Course Design

As you know by now, our objective with virtual instructor-led training (VILT) is to make it as close an equivalent to a physical classroom experience as possible. However, when it comes to instructional design, there are differences between the in-person and virtual courses.

Effective VILT course design requires an intentional and deliberate focus on shaping content for virtual delivery. This includes:

- Chunking the content so it can be easily absorbed
- Sequencing the content in the right order to enable learning and drive engagement
- Designing breakout exercises
- Providing experiential learning assignments and activities between sessions
- Blending self-paced e-learning content into the curriculum
- Using on-screen media appropriately

131

The most effective design methodology is a blended *chunk, sequence, and layer* approach. Blending is the most powerful training modality because it combines multiple learning elements to facilitate knowledge transfer, application, and actualization in the real world.

Over the course of this chapter and the next, I'll give you a broad overview of VILT instructional and media design. This is not and should not be considered a comprehensive nor academic look at virtual training instructional design. I'd need to write another entire book to cover every nook and cranny of virtual course design.

I'll cover the key components of effective VILT design and provide enough insight to get you started on your path toward building highly engaging virtual courses. To supplement these chapters, I've included more information on VILT instructional design and links to design resources on this book's companion website at: https://www.salesgravy.university/vt. Just use the code from the introduction to access these resources for free.

Whether you are converting an existing classroom-based curriculum to a virtual training curriculum or building a VILT from the ground up, keep in mind the two biggest complaints from learners about virtual training:

1. Uncomfortable silence and awkward pauses
2. Lack of engagement

It is important to keep in mind that with virtual training, there are more moving parts for the trainer. The more complex the coursework, the more likely there will be awkward pauses. Therefore, rule number one is to keep it simple. Be very careful not to over-engineer the training structure and content. With virtual training, complexity is your enemy.

So far in this book, I've used the words *engage, engaged,* or *engaging* more than 60 times. I've done this on purpose. When learners are *doing,* they are *engaged.* When they are engaged, virtual training is powerful and often a better choice than physical instructor-led training. When VILT is not engaging, learners check out, the experience is awful, and the course flops.

The keys to designing an engaging virtual course include:

- Keeping sessions short
- Integrating collaborative breakout exercises and role-plays
- Leveraging interactive elements like polls and surveys
- Building multimedia presentation elements into presentation decks
- Incorporating self-paced e-learning elements to extend the learning experience
- Assigning experiential learning exercises and homework between sessions
- Supplementing in-class discussions with instructor facilitated intra-class discussion groups
- Giving learners access to the trainer between sessions for questions, feedback, and coaching

In the virtual classroom, it is super easy for trainers to lose their audience when they are presenting information. It is also easier for trainers to be oblivious to the fact that they've lost their audience.

In the physical classroom, because the trainer can see the entire picture, it is easier for them to read the room and change their pace, boost interaction, or even take a break when engagement wanes. The trainer is much more likely to get signals that they need to stop talking and engage learners. For this reason, good VILT design breaks content into small chunks punctuated by interactive exercises and discussion. This approach keeps learners active and gives the trainers regular signals about learner engagement, which allows them to make adjustments when needed.

Converting Existing Training to Virtual

For most learning and development organizations the first focus is converting existing classroom-based training, in whole or part, to

VILT. This process can often be a bigger challenge than developing virtual training from scratch.

Course conversion requires you and your team to rise above your biases for how the training should be delivered. You'll have to set aside assumptions based on your past experience and get beyond the natural "this is how we've always done it" or "this won't work in a virtual classroom" mental roadblocks. Therefore, when converting existing training to VILT, it helps to begin with an open mindset that is accepting of new possibilities.

Instead of simply trying to shoehorn classroom-based training into virtual delivery, effective conversion requires you to:

- Determine an appropriate course and session length
- Chunk the content so it can be easily absorbed
- Reconsider the sequence of modules
- Layer the content
- Blend elements
- Rework breakouts and role-plays
- Develop new homework exercises
- Prioritize content and eliminating superfluous course content
- Redesign slides for on-screen viewing

Course Length

No matter how you slice it, it takes longer to deliver training in the virtual classroom than in the physical classroom. There are many reasons for this. For example, our Coaching Ultra-High-Performance course requires 12 hours of instruction in the physical classroom, but 16 hours in the virtual classroom; and that's even after shifting some of the content from the classroom-based course to self-paced modules.

For this reason, you must be ruthless when deciding which content stays, which goes, and what can be moved to self-paced modules. I find this exercise to be incredibly helpful because it forces you to tighten up the content and focus on what matters most, which benefits both the virtual training and future classroom-based training.

Session Length As you design virtual training or convert classroom-based training to virtual, consider the length of each session in the course. Because people aren't traveling in to take the course in a physical classroom, you may choose any session length you prefer—60 minutes, 90 minutes, 120 minutes, and so on. And, of course, having half-day or full-day sessions is still an option. We have clients that prefer three- to five-hour sessions, and a few who've scheduled full days of virtual training.

When determining a session's length, it's important to remember that longer sessions are hard on the participants and the trainer. I don't recommend extending sessions beyond the three-hour mark. Should you choose longer sessions, add a 15-minute break every 90 minutes.

My training team at Sales Gravy delivers, on average, over 1,000 hours of virtual training each month. After completing thousands of hours of virtual training, we've learned that 120-minute sessions are optimal: *the Goldilocks zone of virtual training.*

Two hours (120 minutes) is just long enough to cover most modules in a single session, while integrating interactive breakouts, exercises, and role-plays to keep learners engaged. Because these short sessions maximize learning and engagement without taking participants out of the field for too much of the workday, leaders are more likely to buy-in and support the training.

One of the biggest issues with virtual training sessions is that course designers often attempt to cram too much content into a single session. I have done it myself, and it results in a terrible learner experience as the trainer rushes through the slides just to get them all in. Trust me, learners hate this, and you'll see it in their feedback on post-course surveys.

Of course it's common to include too much in a session with physical classroom training, too. When that happens, we have lots of

ways to manage a packed session. Since classroom sessions tend to
last for a day or more, it is easier to move content around, shorten
breaks, or make up time by cutting breakouts shorter. Trainers do
not have any of these luxuries in the virtual classroom. Consequently, it is imperative that the course designers adjust expectations, test assumptions, reduce complexity, and let go of content
that is not mission critical.

Chunk the Content

Virtual training is the perfect modality for chunking high-quality
interactive curriculum. Chunking, similar to Richard E. Myer's
Segmentation Principle,[1,2] breaks complex curriculum into short,
concise virtual sessions.

Rather than the firehose-in-the-mouth format necessitated
with physical classroom training, virtual training opens up the
opportunity to learn the way humans learn best—in short, sequential chunks of information that layer one lesson upon another for
repetition.

For example, an eight-hour physical classroom training might
be delivered (sequenced) in eight 1-hour or four 2-hour sessions
with time in between for practice, homework assignments, and self-
paced e-learning.

Chunking the content into small bites makes it much easier for
learners to consume new information. Numerous academic studies
have proven that humans retain and are more able to apply learned
skills in the real world when training is delivered in succinct, easy-
to-consume chunks.

Learning outcomes improve further when there is time between these chunks of training for participants to practice new
skills in the real world. These breaks between training sessions provide a faster feedback loop that accelerates the cognitive process of
learning. This form of on-the-job experiential learning—learning

by doing—followed by instructor coaching is impractical with most classroom-based training.

The ability to chunk content into short, high-intensity sessions spaced out over time is what makes virtual instructor-led training such a powerful learning experience that results in better long-term learning outcomes. This is exactly why the VILT modality is often superior to classroom training for making learning stick.

Chunking for Ongoing Training   Because many skills are perishable over time, it makes sense to have learners come back to training to refresh and renew them. One-and-done training is rarely effective with making learning stick.

One training tactic that we have deployed successfully to support ongoing training is to turn individual modules of larger virtual courses into deep dive, interactive workshops. These short 120-minute refreshers are easy to deploy, support field coaching efforts, and help keep skills sharp.

VILT Sequencing

Charles Reigeluth's elaboration theory posits that training is more likely to stick when modules and concepts are sequenced in ever increasing complexity with each module layering on, or *elaborating*, on the previous ones.[3]

Therefore, it is important to sequence the training content in the most appropriate order for learning. Lessons and modules should be delivered in a logical, easy-to-follow order that connects the dots for learners.

The sequence of the lessons, modules, and sessions should link to one another creating continuity and flow. Choppy content, complexity, and illogical connections impede knowledge transfer and damage the learner experience.

The key is building sequences of content that make it easy for learners to consume and assimilate new knowledge so that it sticks.

- Start with contextual lessons that flow into deeper content and hands-on learning.
- Start with general overviews that lead to specific, below-the-surface lessons.
- Start with basic building blocks and use them to reach complex frameworks.

I've found that it takes intention, experimentation, and testing/piloting to perfect course content sequences.

The VILT Sequencing Caveat

At Sales Gravy, we learned early on that there is one important caveat to developing virtual course content sequences.

Traditionally, classroom-based courses are designed so that the first modules lay the foundation for learning—what will be taught and why it matters to the learners. These modules require the trainer to spend a great deal of time explaining and talking. This foundational content and learner preparation is a core element of instructional design and it is present in most training curricula.

However, when our trainers delivered foundational material at the beginning of virtual courses, following the same sequence as in the physical classroom, learners checked out. Worse, they walked away from the first session having confirmed their bias that virtual training is a boring and bad experience. They were not motivated to come back for more.

Data from participant surveys and the drop-off in learner participation rates confirmed that placing the traditional foundational content at the very beginning of VILTs was negatively impacting the virtual learning experience.

For this reason, we moved more engaging content up in the sequence. This content required learners to participate, interact, and get hands on at the very beginning of the course. It seemed counterintuitive but it worked.

For example, in one course we moved the module on the telephone prospecting framework up to the first session from the third. Even though this new sequence didn't exactly follow the order we envisioned, it let us kick off with a module that learners really loved. The result was higher engagement for the remainder of the course.

Moving engaging content up in the sequence:

- Caused learners to lean in and it hooked them on the course.
- Quickly dispelled their preconceived notions that virtual training was boring, and that the trainer would just be talking at them.
- Instilled positive behaviors early by teaching learners that they would be required to be alert and participate.

For this reason, it is better to kick off a virtual course with an introduction that grabs attention, followed by interactive exercises that get learners engaged as quickly as possible.

I am a big fan of level-setting exercises in the first few minutes of training. In these exercises, learners go into breakout groups and discuss their biggest challenges (linked to the training focus). This gets them engaged and allows them to get issues, concerns, and complaints off of their chest and on the table.

This does not mean that foundational content that sets up the course is not important. Adult learners still need to know what they'll be learning, why it matters, and the outcomes they can expect. We still need to prepare them to learn.

When there is essential background and foundational content that we need to deliver, but it has the potential to bore learners in a virtual setting, we've found that we can provide this content in two different ways: First, we can use it as pre-work in the form of easy-to-consume, self-paced e-learning modules and exercises. Second, we can integrate small chunks of it into each session over time rather than dumping it onto learners all at once.

Layering

When designing virtual modules, treat them as interconnected lessons that layer, one upon another, rather than independent modules taught under the umbrella of a course title.

Layering is the process of bringing back lessons and concepts from earlier modules and connecting or linking them to the present lesson, role-play, or interactive breakout. It's about repetition.

Adults learn best when they:

1. See the concept on-screen.
2. Hear the instructor describe the concept.
3. Discuss it in collaborative breakout discussions with other learners.
4. Do it through role-plays and real-life practice.

Because repetition is the mother of learning, it is critical that designers and trainers intentionally loop back to content so that learners encounter new concepts again and again within these four learning modalities.

Layering may be accomplished through:

- Summaries of previous lessons at the beginning of each session
- Homework assignments
- In-class polls and surveys
- Self-paced, supplemental e-learning
- Learner reports on how they practiced new skills in the field in session
- Collaborative discussion groups
- Pulling elements of past lessons into breakout sessions and role-plays
- Instructions on how past lessons link to current lessons and why it matters
- Layering questions about previously taught concepts into assessments and quizzes

Integrating Interactive Elements

When it comes to virtual training, the more interactive elements the better. Learners are happiest and most engaged when they are talking and doing. Learners love breakouts, exercises, role-plays, and in-class discussions. Attention spans contract when the trainer is speaking. Therefore, effective virtual training design minimizes trainer broadcasting and maximizes active learner involvement.

My philosophy on training is that real learning occurs in the breakout sessions, role-plays, and intra-class assignments. Thinking through and building these interactive elements into your virtual training courses is the real art of virtual training instructional design. The good news is most modern-day videoconferencing platforms make it super easy to facilitate collaborative breakout sessions.

A good rule of thumb is to have two collaborative breakouts or role-play sessions of 10–20 minutes each per hour. The key is adding more interactive elements that increase learning engagement and knowledge transfer while reducing overall trainer talk time.

Role-Play, Practice, and Experiential Learning   Trainers may teach concepts—show and tell—yet without immediate application (doing it), new knowledge and skills quickly dissipate. The return on training investment is put at risk when learners are not given the time to practice new skills.

The most effective means of facilitating long-term behavior change and skill adoption is to have learners practice the concepts they have learned through hands-on exercises. This can be accomplished with:

- Role-play exercises
- Facilitated practice exercises
- Doing it in the real world, on the job

Experiential learning is more likely to stick when it is accompanied by real-time coaching and feedback.

Leveraging the Learning Management System

From the beginning, we've leveraged our learning management system (LMS) to house, manage, control, and deliver virtual instructor-led training. The LMS makes it much easier to blend and integrate live sessions with:

- Instructions and training for accessing the virtual classroom
- Self-paced modules
- Live session recordings for replay
- Trainer "office hours" and Q&A
- Collaborative discussion groups
- Documents and downloads
- Exercises and assignments
- Assessments

In addition, the LMS improves security, the distribution of learner notifications, management of videoconferencing tools, and tracking and reporting.

Most importantly, the LMS facilitates creating a professional-level learning experience that sends a powerful message to learners and leaders. While you can certainly run virtual training sessions in a webinar-style format, in which you set up a meeting instance on your videoconferencing platform, send an invite to learners, and deliver the session on the platform independent of other learning elements, it is not optimal.

Frankly, it cheapens and devalues the learning experience. Just look around you. Free webinars abound. We sign up for them easily and, more often than not, fail to attend. Maybe we'll watch the replay, but it is unlikely. There is little perceived value or emotional investment.

In similar fashion, it is likely that your organization's leadership conducts regular informational meetings using the same webinar style. People log in so that they are counted on the roster, and immediately check out.

This is exactly why I am not a fan of webinar-style virtual training. Instead, we design formal virtual training courses inside our LMS and leverage it to deliver a complete learning experience.

Facilitator Guides

Trainer facilitator guides must also be developed or revised specifically for virtual classroom delivery. When possible, develop a detailed, step-by-step manual for instructors that shows them exactly how to conduct each individual session of the virtual course. Include an instructor checklist, lesson planning guide, prompts for each lesson and slide, instructions for interactive elements, and expectations for interacting with participants on the LMS discussion groups along with pre-, post-, and intra-course communication with participants.

Building Virtual Training from Scratch

I find that developing new virtual training from scratch is much easier because you are working with a blank canvas and there are fewer legacy issues (e.g., "this is how we've always done it") to deal with. However, because the new course development process requires you to involve multiple stakeholders, it can take longer and be more tedious—especially for creative types.

When building virtual training from scratch, start with the most important question: *Why?* When you are able to answer this question and identify the learning outcomes everything is easier. Start with "why" and let it guide you through the key stages of virtual course creation:

- Needs assessment
- Alignment
- Design
- Implementation and optimization
- Operationalization

Needs Assessment

In the needs assessment phase of creating a new virtual course, your goal is to gather information on the current state of learner competencies and the desired future state. This is the gap your course is aiming to bridge. To tailor the course content to meet organizational needs, you will analyze:

- Competency and skill gaps
- The performance metrics that matter
- Desired curriculum criteria
- Existing training material and modalities
- How learning outcomes will be measured

You'll typically gather this information through stakeholder interviews with executives, managers, participants, and external stakeholders like customers.

The primary questions you should answer before moving to the next step are:

- Can the desired outcome be achieved through training?
- What will happen if the new training program is not deployed?

You'll also want to conduct a technology and environmental analysis to determine if there may be roadblocks related to technology, security, device type, location, bandwidth, time zone, or language gaps that could impede virtual training.

Alignment

Once the initial needs assessment is complete, the next step is gaining alignment from all stakeholders on an outline of training curriculum, desired learning outcomes, and how those outcomes will be measured. This ensures that all stakeholders are on the same page before investing time and resources on course design. It's important to get alignment on the following:

- **Purpose and objective of the training.** "When learners complete this program, what should they know, feel, and be able to do?"
- **The *metrics that matter*.** What are the expected outcomes and how will they be measured? Learning objectives should be strongly connected with learners' on-the-job results.
- **Training modalities.** How should various training modalities be blended to achieve the objective?
- **Overview of curriculum modules.** What are the sub-objectives *for each module?*
- **Critical learning pivot points.** What are the most important things participants must learn and master? It is on these pivot points that we build breakouts, role-plays, exercises, discussion groups, and experiential homework assignments. (Use this same methodology when converting physical training to VILT.)
- **Sequence.** In which sequence will the modules be delivered?
- **Number and length of virtual sessions.**
- **Trainer training.** How will trainers will be trained and what is the roll-out plan for that?
- **Pilot sessions.** Will there be pilot sessions to test the new content? What will be the process for addressing pilot feedback?
- **Technology.** What delivery platforms and LMS will be used?
- **Delivery and deployment.** How, when, and where will the new training be delivered and deployed? Who will deliver it and who will receive it?

Typically, alignment is facilitated with a written plan and proposed training outline based on the information discovered during the assessment phase.

Design

In the design phase, you will build and craft all of the elements of the curriculum in collaboration with subject-matter experts (SMEs). This is the creative step in which you'll leverage a validated instructional design framework and the essentials of good VILT design to build engaging training that achieves the stated objectives.

Implementation and Optimization

In the alignment phase, you set the expectations with stakeholders. Now, you will optimize the curriculum before wider delivery to all learner cohorts. It is exceedingly rare that you deploy the perfect training program right out of the gate. Once the training is delivered in the real world with real learners, you'll find holes in your assumptions, problems with sequencing, curriculum elements that don't work or make sense to learners, and parts of the training that drag and are unengaging. This is exactly why you should begin new training rollouts with pilot groups.

In order to optimize the material, you'll need to examine feedback from learners, trainers, and leaders. You'll look at this alongside outcome-driven metrics from the pilot, which will help you understand how well the course content is fulfilling the established objectives. Once this has all been analyzed, you should have a good understanding of what changes to make to optimize the curriculum.

Operationalization

Once the curriculum, media, technology, and training modalities have been optimized, you will fully integrate the course's language, concepts, frameworks, skillsets, and mindsets into the organizational culture. This phase focuses on imbedding the training into work-flows and toolkits so integration is seamless. This critical step is the key to converting new competencies into long-term performance improvement, cultural transformation, and ROI.

19 | Media
and Visuals

I have no doubt that you've sat through a virtual training or online presentation that was excruciating. A voice droning on and on over heavily bullet-pointed, hard-to-read slides.

Thinking back, it's probably hard to remember anything you learned—but you know that it was boring. Somewhere in the middle, you quit paying attention and started playing on your phone. Sadly, this is exactly how many virtual presentations are formatted and delivered. And this is what learners expect.

In the last chapter you learned that knowledge transfers when learners:

1. See the concept on-screen.
2. Hear the instructor describe the concept.
3. Discuss it in collaborative breakout discussions with other learners.
4. Do it through role-plays and real-life practice.

(Notice how I layered this concept.) Since the learning process begins with seeing, at the heart of virtual instructor-led training (VILT) course design are impactful, engaging, easy-to-consume on-screen visuals that capture attention and pull learners in.

The good news is you can easily develop engaging and memorable virtual training presentations that wow learners and keep them engaged. You just need to be intentional and follow a few important rules.

This begins with a focus on developing slides for an on-screen environment. You must consider various devices, how visuals appear on-screen, and potentially fleeting bandwidth. The objective, of course, is to deliver the best possible learning experience while keeping participants engaged.

Effective visual design sets the tone for the course while conveying a sense of professionalism and clarity.

When we first began delivering virtual training at Sales Gravy, we used the same slides in the virtual classroom as we did in the physical classroom. We gave no thought to the way the slides looked on-screen. But as we began to focus on the Virtual Learning Experience (VLX) in earnest, we changed our perspective.

This began with viewing our visuals through the eyes of learners and we didn't like what we were seeing. Though our overall slide design was okay, the slides themselves didn't pop on-screen. That's when we began a wholesale redesign of all of our virtual training decks. The impact was immediate. Learners gave us incredible feedback and our clients loved the new design scheme.

In this chapter I'm going to share with you the basic design rules that we now follow. They've changed everything for us. Because this is such a deep subject, there is no way to fit everything about slide design in a single chapter. I have included a list of additional visual design resources at this book's companion resource portal: https://www.salesgravy.com/vt. Remember to use code VTB2021X when you check out to gain free access to these resources.

Reduce Visual Noise

The name of the game is reducing visual noise. Visual noise is anything on the slide that impedes comprehension, focus, or connecting with the trainer or content. This problem manifests in many ways, including too much information on one slide, bedazzled graphics, and poorly applied animations and transitions.

When your on-screen visuals are hard to see, stuffed with too many animations, or crammed with too much information, they create cognitive overload. As you've learned, the harder your learner's brain has to work to read and comprehend your presentation, the more likely they will be to tune you and your training message out.

The most effective VILT presentation slides contain a relevant image paired with minimal but meaningful text. The visual design facilitates learning and knowledge retention.

The colors, fonts, images, animations, and transitions should never steal the show. The slides are meant to support the training, not carry it. The slide should act as a billboard that pulls learners in while the instructor drives the interaction and conversation. In other words, the slides are the track, and the instructor is the train.

Presentation Slide Deck Layout

Before designing slides, develop a training presentation template. You are guaranteed to move much faster if you build your template in advance. As you consider your template, keep in mind that the most important key to making your on-screen visuals memorable is to keep it simple and visible.

The layout should result in slides that are clear, easy to read, and readily comprehensible. The style and design should be seamless and consistent, even across different slide layouts. There should be an artistic balance of headlines, images, and content that keeps learners engaged and interested in the training.

Slide Types

Utilizing a consistent design for different types of slides looks polished and eases your learners' cognitive load (Figure 19.1). Begin with a list of the different types of slides you'll create for your deck. For example:

- Title Slide
- Module Title Slides
- Introduction Slides (Course and Module)
- Text Plus Image Slides
- Video Embed Slides
- Framework, Illustration, and Instruction Slides
- Breakout Exercise and Assignment Slides

When the visual design includes slide styles that correspond with what the learners should be doing and what is expected of them—listening and reading, taking notes, asking questions, participating in breakout discussions, working in breakout exercises—you reduce both confusion and friction. Thus, your visual design facilitates learning.

For example, we use a consistent slide design for breakout exercises across all of our courses. When the instructor clicks to that slide type, learners know exactly what to expect. Having a standard slide that specifies the activity type, duration, and a brief description ensures that learners actively participate and reduces the time it takes to prepare them for the exercise.

Style Guide

Next, create a design style guide for each slide type. Your style guide will be a lot like the branding guides marketing organizations build

Examples of slides developed specifically for delivering on-screen in virtual training:

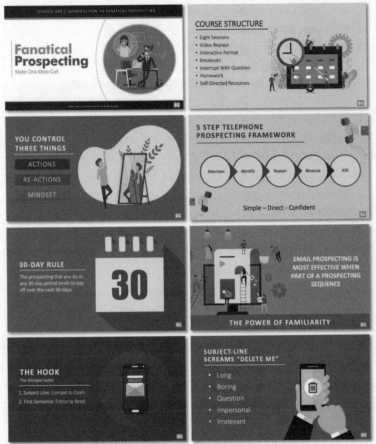

Figure 19.1   Slide Examples

for companies. These guides set the rules for how graphics and text may be used, including:

- Color palette
- Fonts
- Headline font size

- Body font text sizes
- Bullet point styles
- Image size and placement
- Graphics size and placement
- Iconography
- White space and padding (use a grid to facilitate)

Leveraging white space and padding is one of the keys to creating designs that appear professional, uncluttered, and more visually appealing. It's always easy to spot amateur design by simply observing the use and arrangement of white space.

White space is any area on your slides that is devoid of text and graphics. This includes the padding, or blank space, at the top, bottom, and sides of your slides, text boxes, images, and graphics. You'll also want to include spacing between lines and even letters.

White space should be carefully considered and incorporated through the presentation because it plays an important role in making text and images stand out, making them easier to comprehend.

The easiest way to ensure the symmetrical incorporation of white space is to set grids or guides in your slide template. Just go to View and select Guides in PowerPoint to turn this feature on. You'll also want to set a standard for padding on text boxes and between text and graphics. Using the grid system helps you ensure that visual elements are arranged proportionally and are aligned properly.

Good media design and consistency has always mattered for classroom-based training. It matters more in virtual training. It will take additional work and planning to build and perfect your visual style guide, but it's a worthwhile investment of time and effort. Once you've developed it, everything gets easier.

It will make your future design decisions much simpler. And having a design template ready to go will increase efficiency when converting or building new VILTs.

Things also get easier for your learners and trainers, because all of your organization's virtual courses will have a unified look and feel. The consistent visual design allows them to focus on the content, which helps you deliver a legendary virtual learning experience.

Choosing Images

When I'm designing a course, I literally spend hours choosing images. In fact, this is typically the most time-consuming part of the process. I make the investment of time because it is that important.

Scientific studies have proven that humans are much more likely to remember a picture than words.[1] This is why a picture is worth a thousand words—literally.[2]

A relevant, memorable image is a powerful instructional tool that drives learner engagement and reduces cognitive load. The images you use in a course are as important as the text and every other part of the instructional design. Memorable matters because when participants remember, they retain—and when they retain, they learn.

Images also make it easier for your audience to consume your virtual presentation. The human brain processes images 60,000 times faster than text.[3]

Pairing the right image with the message on each slide is critical for making slides relevant and engaging to learners. This is because the message is carried by the text, the image, and the trainer's voice. All three work in unison to make the message memorable.

When choosing images:

- Focus first on the message you want to convey.
- Consider the emotions you hope to evoke.
- Identify mindset shifts you want to provoke.
- Think about what will cause learners to respond and lean in.
- Make sure that the image aids in learning and does not distract.

- Consider how the image will look on the slide and on-screen.
- Ensure that the image pairs well with the text.
- Choose images that are diverse and representative of your audience.
- Use a variety of images (avoid using the same image twice) to keep things fresh.

You'll also want to choose images that look good even when participants are experiencing bandwidth issues. Avoid complex, textured images with gradients. Keep it simple.

When choosing images, remember copyright laws. Don't steal. Just because the image is on the internet doesn't mean that you have the automatic right to use it for commercial purposes. To stay out of trouble, your best course of action is to purchase your images from a stock image provider.

Pair Images with Words

The most impactful slides will consist of images paired with text. Your carefully chosen images and the words you pair with those images should be complementary and balanced.

The process of pairing images with words to more effectively convey your message is a core part of good VILT presentation design. Doing this well requires intention, patience, thoughtfulness, and time.

The data on how words and pictures work together to facilitate learning are overwhelming. The right text paired with the right images have been proven to aid in learner retention and recall.

Text and Fonts

The fastest way to either destroy or improve your visual design is with text and fonts. Poor use of text and fonts is where the biggest mistakes with virtual training presentation design occur.

Minimize Word Count

Mistake number one is cramming too much text on slides. To get it all on one slide, people often reduce the font size. The result is slide content that is very hard for learners to read and comprehend, which increases the probability that they check out.

Hold yourself to a limit of 60 words of text on any slide. When using bullet points, include no more than seven bullet points per slide, and stay under seven words per bullet point.

Break text into easy-to-consume chunks of one to three sentences or short, impactful bullet points. Remember that less is better. Keeping slides light on text reduces clutter on the page, which reduces cognitive load and improves retention.

Reducing the amount of text on slides is challenging. It's natural to feel like you need to write it all out for learners to understand. Just remember, the slide is there to support the trainer, not take the place of the trainer.

Minimizing text requires a focus on editing. Editing is a learned skill. I've written 13 books and I'm still improving. What I've learned about editing over the years is that great books are built in the editing stage rather than in the writing stage. In the writing stage, the author puts words in. During the editing stage, the message is shaped and made more succinct and easier to consume. This often means that words are taken out. That's the real art of editing. This process is also the key to building great training slides. Build the slides, then remove unnecessary words that add no value. This decreases clutter and enhances student retention.

Visually Appealing Fonts and Sizes

Mistake number two is using hard-to-read text. Both the font and the text size are factors here. The most important thing to remember when building slides for virtual training is that people will be viewing media online and on-screen. Depending on the device, those screens may be quite small.

Fonts that are easiest to read on-screen are from the sans-serif family, including Helvetica, Arial, and Calibri.

Keep font sizes consistent for headlines and body text. Headlines should be 36–48 points and bold. This cues participants where to begin reading and makes it easier for them to understand the focus of the discussion and then move their attention back to the facilitator. Body text should be 20–28 points. The smaller the screen, the larger the text should be, so if you know that most of your learners are going to be using tablets or phones for training, you want the text to be on the larger side.

Finally, keep font colors consistent. Consider what's most readable on the slide background color and use bold or underline for emphasis with body text.

Animations and Builds

Leveraging animations and builds on slides is a way to pull learners in by revealing the text in small sequential chunks. For example, if you have a slide with three concepts, you can show just the first one to begin. As you walk through the lesson, you'll use a build or animation to add the next chunk of text when you reach the appropriate moment.

Should you choose to add builds to slides, keep it minimal. Although animations can be a powerful tool for visual design, far too often they add no value and are purposeless embellishments that distract from the message.

Builds work best when you want to control the conversation and keep participants from getting too far ahead of the trainer. Bullet points work particularly well for this. In this setting, builds also help to keep participants engaged because they want to see what is coming up next.

So much technology is available for building dynamic and even cinematic animations that it is easy to get carried away. While these types of additions can take an in-person presentation to whole new levels, they can derail virtual presentations because of limitations on bandwidth and screen size.

Colors and Slide Backgrounds

One of our early discoveries about virtual training presentation design was that traditional slides with white backgrounds are much harder to read on-screen. So, we switched to a new color palette that leveraged slide background colors that were more friendly to the eye.

We found that by using an array of background colors that complemented our images and message, we were able to better set the emotional tone for each slide and create natural variety that kept learners engaged and paying attention.

Choosing the right color palette is an instant way to create a distinctive and stunning virtual training presentation. Blues and muted pastels tend to be the best colors for on-screen viewing.

- Limit your color scheme to five to seven core colors. Then use lighter and darker shades of those colors for accents, contrast, and slide backgrounds.
- Keep colors and sizes for lines and separators consistent.
- Leverage certain colors for messaging. For example, use one color specifically for breakout exercise slides or instruction boxes.
- Keep text colors as consistent as possible. Choose something that is easy to read against your backgrounds. For example, with darker slide backgrounds, we use white text and with lighter backgrounds, we use dark blue text. We use no other text colors.
- Keep background gradients consistent across the presentation.
- Keep iconography styles and colors consistent.

Variation

While consistency is critically important for keeping presentations clear and easy to consume, it's also important to use variations to help keep your audience engaged:

- Chunk concepts across multiple slides so that the screen is always changing.
- Alternate headlines and image placements from left to right.
- Use animations and builds when appropriate.
- Alternate slide background colors.
- Avoid using the same images twice.
- Use title slides to separate modules and lessons.

Whenever there is a change, it's human instinct to look and identify what that change is and what it means. Learners are more tuned in and engaged when there is an assortment of visuals and the screen is always in motion.

20 | VILT Delivery Preparation

John Steinbeck once said, "I have come to believe that a great teacher is a great artist and that there are as few as there are any other great artists. Teaching might even be the greatest of the arts since the medium is the human mind and spirit."

I believe that teaching is an art form, as much as any other art form. Until recently I believed, like so many others, that this form of art was reserved only for the physical classroom, the one place where my talent for teaching and connecting with learners could be fully realized. I was wrong.

I've discovered that transforming virtual training into beautiful art is just learning to paint with a new brush on a different canvas. It forced me to elevate my craft and be better than I ever was in the physical classroom.

In Chapter 9, I wrote that *good enough is not good enough* in the virtual classroom. For the virtual learning experience to rival that of the classroom experience, your virtual delivery must be completely dialed in, from start to finish.

To deliver a legendary virtual learning experience, you must use every bit of your God-given talent, focus, awareness, and preparation to ensure that each element of your virtual training delivery is aligned. You must be prepared for anything and relentlessly driven to eliminate mediocrity in your delivery.

You are an artist. Therefore the way you deliver virtual training (your craft) is far more important than the curriculum and content you are delivering.

The Virtual Classroom Is Unforgiving

When I was in Boy Scouts, our motto was "Be prepared." Most of the disasters and derailments in my life have occurred when I failed to heed this motto.

In the real world, *preparation* means different things to different people. There are many trainers who diligently invest time preparing to deliver training modules. They care about the mission and their credibility. Sadly, there are other trainers who, through lack of caring or pure ignorance, prepare little and subsequently deliver a poor learning experience.

There are also many talented trainers who are so good that they can briefly look over the material the night before, walk into the physical classroom, and wow students with ease. They are good on their feet and able to assess the situation, size up and flex to their audience, and change up the lesson plan on the fly. When you are talented, enjoy teaching, and know the material, preparing for physical classroom training is easy.

I seriously doubt that you care to read another word about why it is critical that trainers prepare in advance for training delivery. Thousands upon thousands of words have been written about why and how trainers should prepare before walking into the classroom.

But here's the brutal truth: The virtual classroom is unforgiving. No matter how you define preparation, if you fail to adequately prepare yourself for each virtual training delivery, there is a high probability that you will deliver a sub-par virtual learning experience.

Even if you know the material like the back of your hand, even if you are gifted with incredible talent and typically do minimal preparation before walking into a physical classroom, you cannot get away with shortcuts when prepping for a VILT.

Because virtual training sessions are short and move at a different rhythm and pace than physical training sessions, there is little margin for error. You must stick to your lesson plan, keep learners engaged, know the material, and have a live-stream production plan and contingency plans for any number of technical issues that may occur.

Therefore, a failure to plan for virtual training deliveries is essentially a conscious decision to fail.

Lesson Plan Power

When you have a full day or several days to deliver training in a physical classroom setting, getting behind, ahead, or off track carries little risk because you have the luxury of time and space to speed up, slow down, and get back on track.

Virtual training sessions, on the other hand, tend to be short and focused. The speed at which time flies in the virtual classroom often catches trainers who are accustomed to teaching in the physical classroom off guard.

This is exactly why having a structured lesson plan for each session is a must with virtual training deliveries. A solid lesson plan ensures that every moment of time spent with you in the virtual classroom is valuable for your learners.

The lesson plan is your roadmap for each virtual training session. It covers what your participants will learn (training outcomes), how you plan to deliver the material, and how you will keep them engaged with meaningful discussions.

Here are the seven elements of an effective virtual training lesson plan:

1. **Visuals.** Review the session visuals/slides and run through all transitions. Ensure that you understand the key learning objectives for the session.
2. **Engagement.** Develop engagement questions, check for understanding questions, polls, personal stories and anecdotes, and group discussion prompts for each slide or concept.
3. **Exercises.** Review breakouts, in-class exercises, and role-plays. This also includes preassigning breakout groups and role-play pairings.
4. **Whiteboard.** Prepare the session whiteboard. If you use a virtual smart board, add your graphics. If you use a standard whiteboard or flip chart, pre-fill the text on the pages and draw frames. Preparing your whiteboard in advance saves time in class and makes you look smooth and prepared.
5. **Session introduction.** Develop your introduction for the session. This includes your plan for following up on homework and layering in a review of key points from the last session.
6. **Production.** Develop your production and switching plan. If you are working with a producer, review the plan with your producer along with the breakout group pre-assignments.
7. **Timing.** Walk through the timing of each element to ensure that you remain on track during the session, keeping a steady pace and avoiding a mad rush at the end.

As you build your lesson plan, reflect on these questions:

- What is the best way to introduce the session topic?
- Do I clearly understand the topic and objective of the session?
- What is most important for learners to take away from the session?
- Why is it important for the learners to know the concepts covered in the session?
- In what ways can I help learners grasp the new concepts and skills and apply them in the real world?

- How will I connect the dots between what participants learn in the session and interconnect with concepts they have learned in previous sessions?
- In what ways and with what questions might I test my learners' previous knowledge, prejudgments, and misconceptions about the session topic and concepts?
- What parts of the training are critical to cover, and which parts can be skipped or moved to the next session if I run out of time?
- How will I introduce each new concept?
- What questions might I ask to provoke awareness, cause learners to think, create aha moments, trigger discussions, and check for understanding?
- Are there unique ways to explain key concepts that will cause learners to lean in?
- What stories, real-life examples, anecdotes, or analogies might I use to illustrate the concepts and help learners understand?
- What can I do to get learners to engage and keep them engaged?
- What is the most effective way to recap the session?

I cannot emphasize enough the importance of building and reviewing your lesson plan for each session—no matter how many times you've delivered it. This process keeps your mind clear, keeps you on track, and plays a crucial role in delivering a legendary virtual learning experience.

Winging It Is Stupid

With virtual training delivery, winging it is stupid. Wickedly stupid. Murphy's Law states that "anything that can go wrong, will go wrong." When you are delivering virtual training, the things that can go wrong, will—and always at the worst possible time, when you are least prepared to deal with it.

What is most important to understand about virtual training is that even if what goes wrong is not your fault, you will still take the blame. For example, if your learners' internet connection is slow, their computer reboots in the middle of training, they don't understand the technology, can't get their mic to work, or it's Wednesday—no matter the situation, they will blame you.

Then, there is your own stress and anxiety about being on camera, working with videoconferencing technology, video and audio equipment glitches, and the never-ending challenge of getting consistent internet upload speeds. When there is a problem during your delivery, it can be embarrassing and induce panic.

Ten years ago, when I was first beginning to use videoconferencing technology, I scheduled a public training webinar. After advertising it for a month, 1,000 people signed up to attend.

The webinar began without a hitch. Six hundred people joined the live virtual training. About 15 minutes in, I noticed in the chat box that dozens of people were complaining that they could not hear me. I panicked. I felt a wave of embarrassment roll over me as I realized how bad I looked in front of all of those people. My fingers hit the keyboard of my computer, searching for a solution.

As the clock ticked, I couldn't breathe. I tried to think, to troubleshoot, but I couldn't focus. Then, I did the worst thing I've ever done during a virtual delivery. In my panic-stricken state, I accidently ended the meeting for everyone. I still cringe when I think about it.

The biology that drives your neurophysiological and emotional responses when things go wrong during virtual training are powerful. Your pulse quickens, breathing gets shallow, and anxiety increases. It is challenging to maintain composure. Attention control is difficult. It's hard to think. Studies have proven that even your IQ drops in these situations—a big problem when you need 100 percent of your intellectual acuity.

The human brain, the most complex biological structure on Earth, is capable of incredible things. Yet, despite its almost infinite complexity, your brain is always focused on one fundamental responsibility—to protect you from threats so that you remain alive.

Harvard professor and psychologist Dr. Walter Cannon first coined the term *fight-or-flight response* to describe how the brain responds to threats.[1] It's also called the *fight-flight-or-freeze response*. In one circumstance, it can save you from certain death, but in another it unleashes a wave of disruptive emotions that can derail you in a virtual training.

The fight-or-flight response is insidious because it is a neurophysiological response that circumvents rational thought. It triggers the release of neurochemicals and hormones, including adrenaline, testosterone, and cortisol, into your bloodstream to prepare you to either stand your ground and fight or run.

Your heart rate accelerates, skin flushes, and pupils dilate. You lose peripheral vision, your stomach tightens, blood vessels constrict, digestion slows down, and you begin shaking.

To prepare your body to defend itself, oxygen- and glucose-rich blood floods into your muscles. However, since there is only so much to go around, blood is moved from nonessential organs and into your muscles. One of these *nonessential* organs is your neocortex—the rational, logical center of the brain. It turns out that, from an evolutionary standpoint, thinking through your options is not an asset when dealing with threats. You need to move quickly to stay alive.

In the clutches of fight-or-fight, you can't think, you struggle for words, and you feel out of control. Your mind reels, palms sweat, stomach tightens, and muscles become tense. As blood drains from your neocortex, your cognitive capacity becomes that of a drunk primate. Then, like me, you click the wrong button and—*poof*—your virtual training ends in disaster.

Preparation Is the Mother of Confidence and Credibility

The real secret to feeling confident during virtual delivery, elevating your game, and coming across as a credible and knowledgeable trainer is *practice and planning*.

Since that horrible incident 10 years ago, I've sharpened and honed my virtual training skills by delivering hundreds of hours of virtual training. Along the way, I learned that the better I plan, the fewer mistakes I make, the fewer issues I face, and better the experience for my learners.

In Chapter 14, we discussed why directors and producers of TV shows and movies go to such lengths to ensure that audio, lighting, framing, and sets are perfect. Doing so allows them to produce an experience that people enjoy and are willing to pay for.

Remember that, as a virtual trainer, you are always on stage. Learners are observing everything about you. They make judgments about whether they like and trust you based on what they see and hear.

You must not forget that, with virtual learning delivery, you are putting on a livestream show. The details matter. The production quality matters. The emotional experience you deliver matters. Therefore, you cannot wing it. You must be prepared.

Pre-Session Checklist and Contingency Plans

Each time pilots prepare for a flight, they go through a checklist. Just peek into the cockpit of the next commercial flight you board prior to take-off. You will observe that the pilot and co-pilot have a physical book open and are going the through the checklist step by step.

These are professionals with thousands and thousands of hours of flight time. They go through that same checklist on every flight. They can recite it by heart. Yet, they still go through the checklist, the same way, every time. Why? Because if something goes wrong at 30,000 ft, the results can be catastrophic. So, it's better to identify problems while they are on the ground.

This is exactly why you need a checklist for virtual training delivery. Your checklist should cover you end to end and include a contingency plan for when things go wrong. I highly recommend reviewing your contingency plan with learners so that they know exactly what will happen and what to do if you lose audio, visuals, or your internet connection is broken.

Give yourself at least 30 minutes before sessions to run your checklist. When I say checklist, I mean a physical checklist that is printed. Before *every* virtual training delivery, review and check off each item on the list. I've learned the hard way that it is a grave mistake to leave anything to chance with virtual training.

The *discipline* to go through your pretraining checklist prior to each virtual training delivery will eliminate 99 percent of issues that contribute to embarrassing situations. It will ensure that your deliveries go smoothly, you will feel more confidence, and your learners will have a better experience.

Power and Battery Backup

Your checklist should start with *Turn the power on* and *Plug the laptop into power.* These first steps might seem remedial and a blinding flash of the obvious—unless you were with me when my laptop shut down in the middle of a training delivery because I had not plugged it in and the battery died. Or, the time it was plugged into a power strip, but the strip had been inadvertently turned off and my battery died right in the middle of a delivery for an important client.

There are no words to describe how embarrassing these situations were. Because the learners could not see me, they had no idea what happened. If I had been there with them, I would have simply said, "Oops, my battery died; is there an outlet I can plug into?" Instead, as soon as my screen went dark, they were left to make up a narrative about what happened in their own heads.

In both cases, it took me several minutes to get back into the virtual classroom. By the time I got back in, the learners were all gone. They had moved on to other things. In the physical training classroom, trainers are often like guests of the client, but virtual training flips that around, making the trainer the host. This means that your learners are also like your guests, and they're less likely to give you the benefit of the doubt when things go wrong. Everything is on you.

Power is everything. No power, no virtual training.

- Check all cords and connections to ensure that your laptop or device is plugged into power.
- Check the power icon on your laptop or device to ensure that it is receiving power.
- If you are on a fiber internet connection that requires power, check your backup battery to be sure that it is fully charged and working.
- If possible, connect your Wi-Fi router to a backup battery source.
- Ensure that all batteries on devices, mics, cameras, and lights are fully charged. I find that it is a good idea to plug everything in the night before so that you have full charges at the beginning of the day. If you begin your day on empty, you'll be chasing your batteries all day.

I highly recommend investing in a backup power unit. We have everything that uses power on our virtual training sets connected to backup batteries. These units double as surge protectors and have internal batteries that kick on in the event of a power outage so that your training session is not interrupted. Backup batteries have saved us on numerous occasions during storms when the power blinked on and off.

Internet Connection and Backup

Your internet connection is mission critical. It is how you deliver your live video and audio stream. You'll want to do everything in your power to enhance upload speed and plan for contingencies.

Like many people, you may live or work in an area or office where (1) speed and bandwidth go up and down depending on the day, (2) weather impacts speed, or (3) internet speed is poor all of the time. I highly recommend investing in a backup connection source like a mobile hotspot. Having a backup source has saved me on many occasions when my main broadband source went down.

You may also want to consider investing in a broadband connection that is used only for virtual training. In the past, we ran into problems in our office when too many people are uploading large files at the same time. Our solution was to isolate our virtual training studios on their own broadband connection.

- Use an ethernet connection when possible. Check that the ethernet cable is plugged in correctly and you have turned Wi-Fi off on your device.
- If you are using Wi-Fi, check your Wi-Fi signal strength.
- Check your internet upload speed. If it is super slow, try restarting your router and restarting your computer or devices (allow plenty of time before your training session for these resets).
- Turn Wi-Fi off on all devices that are not being used for the training—this includes digital assistants like Google Home and Alexa.
- Make sure people in your household or office are not streaming video, playing games, or uploading files. Even small interruptions in audio and video caused by slow internet speeds can cause learners to have a negative perception of you.[2] Don't take any chances.
- Pause uploads on all file sharing apps like Dropbox, Google Drive, and One Drive. Ask the people in your office to pause uploads as well.
- Close your email application.
- Close browsers and other apps that may be using internet bandwidth in the background.
- Check your backup connection to be sure that it is fully charged, has a good signal, and that your computer or device sees it. Practice connecting to your backup source so that you can do it with one click if your main connection goes down. Check to be sure that your computer or device will connect to this source before your call.

Audio

You've learned that the most important technical element of your video call is audio. Always have a backup microphone tested and ready to go as a contingency. If you use an external mic powered by batteries, buy two and have one fully charged and ready to go just in case your battery dies.

- Check to be sure your mic is connected properly to your laptop, desktop computer, or camera.
- Check to be sure the correct microphone is selected on your videoconferencing platform. *Tip:* If you cannot find your microphone in the videoconferencing microphone settings, it is not connected properly to your device.
- Test volume levels and make adjustments.
- Make sure your microphone is positioned correctly.
- Test output speakers or earphones to be sure you can hear the other party.
- Check batteries in microphones and earphones to ensure they are fully charged.
- Practice switching to your backup microphone or the internal microphone on your computer until you can do it smoothly.

Audio problems happen. It's a fact of life with virtual training. We've found that audio disconnects are more common than internet issues. For this reason, we purchased small whiteboards for our trainers that allow them to jot a quick message to learners asking them to stand by when audio goes out. This puts their learners at ease, giving them the time that they need to switch mics or trouble shoot.

Lighting

Good lighting is the key to looking your best on-screen.

- Check the position of your lights.
- Check brightness and temperature levels.
- Check power connections and backup batteries.

- Check for harsh glares and pull shades on windows to regulate natural light.
- If you are using a virtual backdrop with or without a green screen, check the lighting to ensure that you are not disappearing into the backdrop, discolored, or distorted. You'll need to give yourself plenty of time for this and check it on every call.

Camera

Check camera settings before every call. Give yourself plenty of time. Never leave this to chance. It is embarrassing when you must make camera adjustments in the middle of the call. Always have a backup camera available. This should typically be either the built-in camera on your computer or a spare USB based webcam so that switching on the fly is easy.

- Check to be sure your camera is connected properly to your laptop.
- Check to be sure the correct camera is selected on your videoconferencing platform. *Tip:* If you cannot find your camera in the videoconferencing video settings, it is not connected properly to your device.
- Check color temperature and focus. Be sure that the lighting is set properly so that you look natural and not washed out.
- Check power connections and backup batteries.
- Check your camera position and framing so that the camera is at eye-level, your hands and torso are visible, and you are aligned appropriately on the vertical and horizontal access with no distortion.
- If you are using a green screen, test the key.
- Practice switching to your contingency camera.
- Log in to a test meeting on your videoconferencing platform to test your camera, audio, and lighting. Make a recording and play it back so that you can see and hear yourself from the same perspective as the learners. Give yourself enough time to troubleshoot or shut things down and start back up again if there are problems.

Backdrop

Your backdrop is the heart of your virtual training set. It sends a powerful message. Be sure that it is the message you want to convey.

- Check your backdrop to be sure that everything is in place and it looks good in the video frame. In an active working space, it is not uncommon for your backdrop to be disturbed or moved. If you don't have a permanent backdrop or you have to move it to another area, check it in the frame before your session begins.
- Check to be sure your backdrop is properly lit and that there are no distracting glares or shadows.
- If your backdrop includes a TV monitor or smart board, make sure that it is turned on and the correct image is on the screen.
- If your backdrop includes a whiteboard, make sure that it is erased and clean or has the message you wish to convey.

Platform Settings

Check your videoconferencing platform settings before your virtual training session begins. Just because everything was working on your last session, do not assume that it will work on the next one.

- Check to ensure your app is updated to the latest version.
- Check audio source.
- Check video source and virtual background source if you are using that option.
- Check to be sure you are connecting to the right meeting ID—nothing like you and your learners being in different meeting rooms (I have that T-shirt).
- Check the recording settings, make sure you are recording, and note where that recording will be stored—nothing like forgetting to push record or losing the video after the fact. We've set our platform default to record to keep this from happening.
- Check the video quality settings.

- Check to be sure chat is set to *activated* or *deactivated*, depending on your intentions.
- If you are using a waiting room, be sure you know how to move participants from the waiting room into the meeting.
- Check and practice screen sharing to be sure that you have your windows arranged correctly to make the transition from video interface to screen sharing seamless.
- Check the *join meeting* settings to be sure that people can see and hear you and you can see and hear them when you join.

This is important, so pay attention: If you are delivering training on your client's platform, go to that platform at least an hour *before* your session starts to download any required apps and check audio and camera compatibility settings. Trust me on this; you will likely need to make adjustments, and you do not want to be making those adjustments when the training starts.

Background Noise and Distractions

Background noise like pets barking and alerts from your phone can make you seem unprofessional. Distractions steal your attention, causing you to break eye contact, stop listening, and lose your train of thought.

- Whether you are in the office or at home, make sure everyone around you knows that you are delivering training and that they need to be quiet. A sign on your door at home or at your office is also a good idea. We have ON AIR lights mounted outside all of our virtual training studios. When the light is on, people know to be quiet.
- Isolate pets in an area of your home so that they don't distract you with barking or jump into your set.
- Mute all devices, put them in do-not-disturb mode, and move them away from your line of sight.
- If you are expecting a delivery from UPS or FedEx, put a note on your doorbell asking the delivery person not to use it. If you have a smart doorbell, mute the sound.

Computer Desktop

Many, many trainers have been deeply embarrassed by inadvertently sharing the wrong desktop window or having to dig through the clutter on their desktop to find the correct file to share.

- Close all windows on your computer except the videoconferencing app and visuals you plan to share.
- Put your computer or laptop in do-not-disturb mode.
- Practice the motion of choosing the correct window and sharing your screen several times so that you can do it seamlessly.
- It is never a bad idea to restart your computer prior to training sessions. It will run faster, and updates will process before you join your call.

Physical Appearance

I once did an entire virtual training with my shirt collar on the outside of my jacket—like John Travolta in *Saturday Night Fever*. I didn't notice it until I watched the replay video—another embarrassing moment because I failed to check things beforehand. Before you start the virtual training session, check your hair, teeth, nose, face, and clothing.

Always be camera ready.

21 | Set the Rules

I'm a known rule breaker. I don't like constraints and have always pushed back against rules. Even as I built and grew my company, I eschewed handcuffing my people with rules. I've successfully delivered thousands of hours of in-person training with only two rules for participants:

1. Turn off all devices, including laptops.
2. Come back from breaks on time.

I've rarely, if ever, needed more rules than these to control my classroom and keep things on track. After all, we're dealing with adults and I've always believed that the fastest path to mutual respect is to treat my learners like adults.

Virtual training is different. Here, rules matter. A clear set of rules should be covered beforehand and at the beginning of the training with both participants and their leaders. This approach enhances rather than detracts from the experience.

Rules are needed because virtual training has so many moving parts and, the sad fact is, participants and their leaders don't always give virtual training the same respect and attention that they give in-person training.

Rule One: Virtual Training Is Still Training

The first and most important objective of your virtual classroom rules should be to establish that virtual training is delivered at the same level as physical training and the same expectations apply.

Let's say that you brought in 20 people for an in-person training. At the beginning of class, you ask everyone to turn off their phones. You promise to give them plenty of breaks so that they have time to check email and return calls. Once you set that expectation, it's rare that a participant would take a call from their boss in the middle of class and conduct the call in middle of your classroom.

Not so much with virtual training. If you are not clear and *firm* with both leaders and learners about interruptions, you'll end up with a screen full of people on mute writing emails, talking to other people, answering the phone, and getting pulled away from training by the boss.

Start With the Leaders

Leaders are the top cause of learner interruptions. When learners are attending physical training, it is much more difficult for leaders to pop in and interrupt them. But when learners are in the office on a virtual training session, all bets are off.

Unless you get leaders to buy into removing distractions and interruptions, participants will get pulled away and the learning experience will suffer.

In every case possible, I meet with the leaders my learners work for (typically on a video or audio conference call) and explain the rules. I review my expectations, including those around classroom participation and time commitments for inter-class assignments. It's helpful to do this as we review the class schedule and syllabus together. If I'm unable to arrange a synchronous conversation with the leaders, I send them an email and a video that explains the virtual classroom rules. These are not suggestions; they're clear expectations.

Whenever possible, I encourage leaders to join the virtual sessions as observers and breakout group facilitators. This is much easier to accomplish in a virtual training session than in a traditional classroom.

Getting the leaders involved in virtual training sessions is one of the secrets to making training stick. It works in two ways:

- First, when leaders attend the training as observers, it sends the message to the learners that the course content is important.
- Second, because the leaders are directly engaged, they are more likely to reinforce the training.

Participation helps leaders see the value of virtual training, and when they help with breakouts and role-plays, you tap into their practical experience, which makes your job much easier.

This upfront alignment with the leaders almost always works. Leaders want their people to learn and grow. They also want to get an ROI from the training expense. Once leaders buy in, they work with you to minimize disruptions and ensure that their people are prepared to learn.

Basic Virtual Classroom Rules

In addition to Rule One, *virtual training is still training*, we use a few other simple rules to help learners get the most out of their virtual learning experience.

Tech Check

Participants should do a platform and tech check three days before class starts. This includes successfully logging in and accessing the video conferencing platform, learning management system, and virtual whiteboard. It also is a chance for them to check their video and audio settings. Should anyone have problems, ensure that there is an established process for getting issues resolved—before the training date.

When possible, especially when working with learners that have not attended virtual training before, schedule a group tech check-in. This is a specific time when everyone logs into the video conferencing platform and any issues may be dealt with on the spot. You may also consider recording a how-to video for logging in to the virtual classroom.

Learning Space

Participants should enter the virtual classroom from a quiet space, with minimal background noise and good lighting. Participants are responsible for alerting the people around them that while they are in training, they are not to be disturbed.

Microphones on Mute

Participants should keep microphones on mute unless they are called on. Ensure that people know not to dial in on their phone and use computer audio at the same time because it creates an incredibly annoying feedback loop.

Do Not Disturb

All devices should be turned off. The computer or laptop they are using to enter the virtual classroom should be put in Do Not Disturb mode. Email, web chat, collaboration tools, phones, social media, and so on must be turned off. Virtual training sessions are short. Everything can wait.

Log in 15 Minutes Early

Participants should log into the virtual classroom 15 minutes prior to the class start time. Emphasize that class will always start on time—*and always start on time*. Do not wait for stragglers. The moment you get sloppy with starting class on time, your participants will respond in kind.

We play an animated video on a loop prior to class that reviews class rules (Figure 21.1). There is a countdown clock on the video. We've found that this video helps everyone relax because they know exactly when class begins.

Video / Webcams On

Participants are required to have their cameras on. During training sessions, participants should face the camera. For the virtual classroom to be truly interactive and engaging, you and the participants must be able to see one another. Body language and facial expressions are an essential part of communication. Likewise, virtual training works much better when participants attend on their own device rather than sharing in groups.

Full Names on Screen

Participants are required to use their full name on the moniker placed on their video frame. The name on each video frame is much like a tent card that participants place in front of them during in-classroom training. We have a short video tutorial to show participants how to add their full name to their video frame on the video conferencing platform.

Figure 21.1   Screen shot of countdown video.

Interactive

For virtual training to be engaging, it must also be interactive. Learners are expected to fully participate in breakouts and role-plays. Ensure that you give learners permission to interrupt you with questions.

Pre-Work and Homework Exercises

It's important for participants to complete course pre-work and homework exercises on time. As the trainer, you must hold people accountable for these exercises and review homework with report outs before each session.

The real key to gaining compliance with virtual classroom rules is your personal discipline. You are always on stage, so you set the tone. When you walk the talk, you'll find that learners and leaders quickly fall in line and the virtual learning experience improves for everyone.

22

Controlling the Virtual Classroom

There are three key factors that can affect your ability to maintain control of the virtual classroom:

- Distractions in your participants' environments
- Your attention control and distractions in your own environment
- Disruptive learners and challenging learner communication styles

The keys to maintaining control include the following:

- Set and communicate the rules and expectations up front. See Chapter 21.
- Approach the virtual classroom with relaxed, assertive confidence.
- Keep your training delivery interesting, interactive, and engaging to maintain instructional momentum.

- Focus all of your attention on your learners.
- Effectively manage learner style types that disrupt your classroom.
- Pull attention back to you when learners begin to drift.

Maintaining control of the virtual classroom is imperative for facilitating a safe, interactive, collaborative space where everyone has the opportunity to participate, and you enjoy teaching. It also sets the foundation for learner participation and engagement.

Participant Distractions

The virtual training session was going smoothly. People were engaged, having fun, and getting a lot out of it. Nearly all the participants were connecting from home.

Then, the door behind one participant slowly opened. A small child (the participant's four-year-old son) peeked his head in the door. Then he very slowly entered the room and stood a few feet behind his father.

This happens from time to time in participant video frames along with cats, dogs, birds, and spouses making impromptu appearances. Except that in this case, the child was completely naked and just stood there, transfixed.

His father was so focused on the training that he didn't notice him, but everyone else certainly did. The instructor tried to stay focused and keep moving, but it was clear that she was being upstaged. People were texting each other and sending one another private chats as they tried to look anywhere except at the naked kid.

Awkward doesn't begin to describe it. After several long minutes, much to everyone's relief, the kid crouched down and crawled out of the room. But the damage had been done. There was one main takeaway from that session, and it was all about the kid. Later, when the father learned what happened, he was mortified.

When it comes to controlling the virtual classroom, the biggest disruptors are most likely to come from the individual participants' environment. These can be phone calls, email, text messages, deliveries, the boss, customers, peers, family members, pets, children, or anything else that steals the participants' attention. In some cases, as in the previous story, these disruptors can negatively impact the entire class. This is one of the reasons for participants to keep their microphones on mute most of the time.

Situations like a naked child walking into the room are exceedingly rare, and the most you can do is remain calm and press on. However, when you notice a learner becoming distracted, it's crucial to deploy techniques to compel the participant to refocus on you.

Pulling a learner's attention back to you is a two-step action:

1. Keep a close eye on learner video frames to watch for drift and inattention. (This is one of the key reasons to require that video be turned on.)
2. When you notice that a learner is not paying attention, call on them. Ask a question, ask for their opinion, ask for their feedback. Compel them to respond, then praise them for responding by giving them a positive comment. You don't need to mention that you noticed they weren't paying attention. They'll already know that.

As you do this consistently, your participants will learn that engagement and attention are required in your classroom.

When you allow the little things to slide, it sends the message that it's okay for learners to prioritize other activities over the training session. Soon, more and more participants will start tuning you out and focusing their attention on other things—and it will be nearly impossible to regain control of the session.

Finally, there are rare situations in which the entire group hits a mental wall and begins to lose focus. Sometimes in these situations the vibe turns negative. When that happens, the best move is to take a 10- to 15-minute break to give participants some breathing room and then regroup.

Disruptive Learners and Challenging Communication Styles

Finally, there is the challenge of dealing with disruptive learners. This isn't new because most veteran instructors are accustomed to dealing with difficult participants in the physical classroom. However, working with challenging learners in the virtual classroom can require more finesse.

While learner environmental distractions are the primary cause of control issues in your virtual classroom, certain participant behavioral patterns can disrupt your instructional flow, impede full participation, interrupt learning, and create a negative vibe. Knowing how to spot, neutralize, and redirect these seven learner style types will help you maintain an open and collaborative classroom.

The Grouch

The grouch reveals themselves in one of two ways. You'll either see them in their video frame with arms crossed and a not-so-pleasant look on their face, or they'll come right out and tell you, and everyone in the class, that they don't want to be there.

I recently had an aggressive grouch express in the first few minutes of a course that he believed that virtual training was "bogus and a complete waste of time." He turned out to be one of my best students, but it was tense as all the participants watched to see how I would respond.

When you get punched in the nose by a grouch, you will feel a strong desire to win them over and convince them that the training is in their best interest. But selling them on the training or arguing with them doesn't work. It only serves to feed their negative energy and causes them to dig in and defend their position.

Therefore, the most effective way to win over a grouch is to allow them to express themselves without taking the bait. Ignore their grouchiness and instead get them involved. Pull them into discussions. Call on them often. Praise them for their participation. Compliment them on their answers.

The more grouches are engaged and doing things, the more valuable they will feel, and the less they will think about why they don't want to be in the training. Often, you'll convert them from naysayers to advocates.

The Dominator

The dominator is the learner who seems to already know it all. Typically, the dominator is an experienced person who has been in their position for a long time. In some cases, they are a former manager or trainer, or believe that they have been wrongly passed over for promotions. Dominators usually have an extreme lack of self-awareness.

Dominators will directly challenge you and the concepts you are teaching. They tend to suck all the oxygen out of the virtual classroom, putting their own spin on what you are teaching—often contradicting you. It can feel as if they are actively trying to undermine you and take over the course.

They'll bring up worst-case scenarios. They may implicitly or explicitly say that the concepts won't work. They'll give examples and stories to illustrate their negative points, and this can bring your instruction to a halt. They may even complain that your training is just another flavor of the day.

Imagine, for a moment, if I put a huge piece of rich German chocolate cake in front of you. Your mouth would water. As you dove in, it would taste delicious. But eventually, as with all rich foods, it would fill you up. As you had your fill, it would no longer taste as good or trigger the same ravenous desire.

The key to neutralizing the dominator is feeding their ego until they are full. What the dominator wants most is to feel important. So, tell them they are special and important. Express that you appreciate their experience. Praise them for helping. Ask their opinion. Soon, their ego will fill to the brim. They'll be satisfied and move out of your way.

The Psychology Behind Effectively Neutralizing Grouches and Dominators

Both the grouch and the dominator can trigger a wave of disruptive emotions in you. In some cases, depending on how aggressive they are toward you, they trigger your fight-or-flight response, causing you to either feel deeply insecure or become angry. In either case, it can be difficult to gather your thoughts and control your response.

You may recall our discussion on emotional discipline and emotional contagion from Chapter 7. In that discussion, you learned emotions are easily perceived and transferred from one person to the next, and people respond in kind.

When you get challenged and respond with insecurity, it encourages grouches and dominators to become even more aggressive in their attempts to bully you. They will actively work to exploit any weakness they perceive.

Should you respond with anger or irritation, you give them what they want. You feed their negative behavior, cede your moral authority, and open the door to even more disruptive pushback.

The more you push, the more they'll dig their heels in and resist you. This behavior is called *psychological reactance*. When someone tells you that you're wrong, your response is quick and emotional (even when you really *are* wrong): "Oh yeah? I'll show you!"

Psychological reactance unleashes a person's inner brat. This is the reason you cannot argue other people into believing they are wrong. No matter the logic of your argument, data, or supporting facts, the people you are arguing with will dig in their heels and rebel.

When you trigger reactance, you push the learner away from you rather than pulling them toward you. For this reason, arguing, rebutting, and debating do not work. The truth is, in these tense situations, it is the person who exerts the greatest level of emotional control, who has the highest probability of diffusing the situation and controlling the classroom.

When you respond in kind to grouch or dominator behaviors, you lose and they win. It is fruitless to attempt to out grouch the grouch or push the dominator into a submissive state. However, when you respond with a noncomplementary behavior—relaxed, assertive confidence—you transfer those emotions to your learners, reduce resistance and encourage engagement. In turn, you get more respect and even greater control of your virtual classroom.

The Joker

Much like the dominator, the joker often has an extreme lack of self-awareness. This participant has a tendency to use sarcasm or inappropriate jokes, often at the wrong time.

Most of their jokes fall flat, but the timing can disrupt your flow and ability to effectively make your points. Some of their ill-timed wit introduces negativity into the classroom.

While you feed the ego of the dominator, you do the opposite with the joker. Give them no oxygen. No emotional reaction. No attention. Just ignore them and keep moving.

The joker craves attention. This often comes from a place of insecurity. Once they learn that their joking doesn't create the attention they seek, they'll get the message and stop.

The Eager Pleaser

The eager pleaser is always there, enthusiastically participating. They are engaged, focused, and want to please you.

Eager pleasers answer questions, report out for their breakout groups, and give you positive feedback. They are the first to turn in their homework, participate in every discussion group, and ask for feedback and coaching. They are your biggest advocates.

But the eager pleaser can be a double-edged sword. On one hand, you wish all participants were this enthusiastic and tuned in. On the other hand, they can squeeze out other participants during discussions, slow down course momentum with all of their eager questions, and drain the emotional life out of you with their neediness.

The key to handling the eager pleaser is balance. You don't want to discourage them, but you want to be careful to draw some boundaries. Tactics for managing the eager pleaser include:

- Intentionally rotate the role of breakout group spokesperson to give others a chance to talk.
- When the eager pleaser takes over every discussion, begin calling on other participants by name even when the eager pleaser has their hand up.
- Between class, don't ignore the eager pleaser, but don't respond to every email, text, or phone call immediately. Allow some space and usually, they'll get a clue and dial it back.

The Shy Mouse

The shy mouse's goal is to fly below the radar. They do not like to be in the spotlight.

The shy mouse gladly allows the eager pleaser to take the floor and answer for them. They sit as quietly as possible in an attempt to avoid being called on. They rarely offer an opinion or engage in group discussions.

It is important not to mistake the shy mouse's quiet nature as nonengagement. It's also important to be careful when putting them on the spot. When they feel embarrassed, they'll shut down.

To get the shy mouse more engaged, begin with asking them really easy questions—questions that they can answer without thinking. Always give them positive feedback for sharing—no matter how they answer. Avoid telling them that they are wrong or debating a point with them in front of the group.

Should the shy mouse have difficulty answering a question or be too shy to speak in front of everyone, let them off the hook by throwing the question to another learner.

You'll be most successful at pulling the shy mouse out of their shell during small group breakouts in which they are paired with three to five people. In these small groups the shy mouse doesn't feel as intimidated and is much more likely to get involved and express their thoughts and opinions.

The Top Dog

Because it is so easy for leaders to jump into your virtual sessions, it is not uncommon to get a top dog, or senior leader, showing up in your virtual classroom. Top dogs can both unnerve you and be a distraction for participants, who hold back in the presence of a person with authority.

In the presence of the top dog, you must rise above your own insecurity and exude relaxed, assertive confidence. Be very careful not to change your training style. That's a fast track to inauthenticity and failure. Be your natural, awesome self and teach the course based on your lesson plan.

Still, there is the elephant in the room, and everyone knows it. For this reason, you should engage the leader and give them the floor. Typically, at the start of the session, I'll defer to them and ask if they'd like to address the group. They almost always do, offering positive encouragement, and then, ego satisfied, leave soon after.

If they stick around, get them involved by pulling them into discussions and breakouts. When they participate, the learners gain the value of the top dog's experience, and you gain an advocate. Likewise, getting them involved humanizes them, thus reducing learner anxiety.

There is one important caveat, though. If you notice that the top dog is not paying attention, do not call on them. Doing so may embarrass them and be a career-limiting move for you.

The Distanced Learner

Perhaps the biggest challenge is the distanced learner—the person who is logged into your virtual classroom but is not there in spirit. The distanced learner is essentially checking the box and getting an attendance credit without actually participating and learning.

They'll turn their camera on and off periodically during the training as they leave to focus on their priorities. When they are on camera, they'll be on phone calls, clearly working on other things, or having conversations with people in their space who are just off camera.

When you call on them to pull them back in, they don't respond because they cannot hear you. They have you on mute.

When dealing with the distanced learner, step one is scheduling an offline conversation with them. My typical move is to leverage a takeaway. I'll say something like: "I notice that you are really busy with other things; perhaps now is not the right time for you to take this training. Why don't we reschedule you?" In many cases, this is all it takes to get them back on track.

If this doesn't get their attention, I'll call their leader and ask for help. But be careful if you decide to escalate things. Should the leader come down hard on the person, the distanced learner will blame you and may quickly transform into a very hard-to-manage grouch.

What you cannot do is allow this mediocre behavior and lack of discipline to infect the other participants and become contagious. For this reason, if you have no other options than to ignore their behavior, hide their video frame from view so that no one can see them.

Attention Control and Being Present

The late Jim Rohn said, "Wherever you are, be there." This is essential advice when it comes to virtual training. To keep learners engaged, you must be present in the virtual classroom.

In the words of author Myrko Thum: "The present moment is the only thing where there is no time. It is the point between past and future. It is always there, and it is the only point we can access in time. Everything that happens, happens in the present moment. Everything that ever happened and will ever happen can only happen in the present moment. It is impossible for anything to exist outside of it."[1]

Being present means not being distracted by past regrets or future worries and instead being centered on the here and now.

It is being focused, aware, and mindful in the moment. This, of course, is much easier said than done. We've all been jolted out of the moment by a ding from our phone, a notification on our computer screen, or a person delivering a message that yanks our attention away from the moment to some other place.

If you've ever been in a conversation with another person and they've looked away, become distracted, or interrupted your conversation to return a text message or email, you know how disrespected it makes you feel. When you don't feel like the other person is listening to you, it hurts your feelings, makes you feel unimportant, and can cause you to become angry.

In today's demanding work environment, it is easy for trainers to become distracted. We are constantly looking at our devices. Phone calls interrupt conversations. Email, text messages, and social media distract us. Because participants are on-screen rather than right in front of you, it is much more challenging to stay focused on them. But if you want to be in control of your training, you need to be focused on your learners.

Remaining focused requires intentional attention control. The best way to prevent yourself from getting distracted is to make a deliberate choice to remove distractions. You can do this with a few changes to your virtual training environment. I recommend these strategies:

- Let the people in your office or home know that you are delivering training and are not to be disturbed.
- Block your calendar so that people know that you are in a training session.
- Put a sign on the door to your training room to let others know that you're training.
- Place your phone and computer in "do not disturb" mode.
- Turn the sound off on all devices so that beeps, dings, and buzzes don't cause you to look away.
- Plan your training so everything you need is readily accessible.
- Keep your eyes off papers and other screens to avoid the burning desire to multitask.

The moment you make the mistake of looking away from the camera and your class, you lose concentration and break eye contact. Controlling your eyes keeps you there and in the moment. *As go your eyes, so goes your attention.*

When you're tempted to take a peek at your inbox, phone, or even out the window, remind yourself that whatever is tugging at your attention can wait. After all, if you expect learners to give you their undivided attention, hold yourself to the same standard.

Once you've neutralized distractions, you need to keep your focus sharp. This can be tough work, especially after spending so much time on video, which can make you feel drained and diminish your willpower. *Zoom fatigue* is a real problem.[2]

Two things happen when you zone out during virtual training. The first is that it makes it more difficult for you to stay in an authoritative position. You don't notice distracted participants. You forget what you were about to do or say. The energy level dips, and everyone can sense it. This is when your learners' attention also starts slipping away, and you might not even notice. When you finally do, it's that much harder to pull their attention back to you.

The second thing that happens when your attention drifts is that you miss crucial information. Often, you end up asking learners to repeat themselves or ask questions that have already been answered. This is especially damaging to learner engagement and the learning experience. It's proof that you were not listening, which destroys your credibility, makes learners feel insignificant, and causes them to disengage.

Attention control is similar to impulse control. It's sacrificing what you want *now*, like checking Facebook for the latest cat video, for what you want *most*, connecting with your learners, making an impact, and achieving your mission. Maintaining attention control and remaining in the moment while you are in the virtual classroom sets the stage for maximizing learner engagement and delivering a legendary virtual learning experience.

23 | VILT Communication Plan

With virtual training, learner confusion is your enemy. Learners and their leaders will be confused about:

- How and where to log into the virtual classroom platform
- How to use the features of the platform
- How to log into and use your learning management system (LMS)
- Technology and videoconferencing equipment
- Class times and lengths
- Rules and expectations for engaging in the virtual classroom
- How to engage in breakout sessions
- How to use the virtual whiteboard or smart board (if you incorporate this type of technology into your sessions)
- Homework and between-session assignments, and how to post them

- Post-coursework and follow-up
- And a dozen other things you never dreamed might possibly confuse people

What is critical to understand is that, unlike with physical training, when delivering virtual training learners and their leaders will blame anything that goes wrong on you, even if it is not your fault. This includes their own issues with internet connections, microphones, cameras, user error, and failure to read the instructions.

When they are having difficulty accessing information, getting into your session, or even getting online, they'll point their fingers at you as the culprit. For this reason, consistent, clear, communication helps you to both gain the moral high ground and minimize issues.

We've learned that the more our trainers communicate, the more we neutralize confusion and improve the experience for learners. There are three keys to breaking though confusion:

1. **Overcommunicating.** With virtual training, one-and-done communication does not work. Develop and execute a systematic ongoing communication plan, in advance, for every virtual course you teach. Even when you feel like you are communicating enough, you probably are not.
2. **Clear and concise communication.** Review it once, review it twice, and be sure that anyone who reads, listens, or watches it will understand exactly what you are communicating. Keep your message direct and brief.
3. **Being available.** Make sure that learners have easy access to you for questions and troubleshooting—and be responsive. In situations where you are not available, ensure that learners have an alternate contact point.

Your virtual training communication plan for each delivery should:

- Get important information in the hands of learners early and often.
- Remove excuses for not having the information or understanding the information.

- Build emotional connections with learners.
- Get learners engaged early.
- Create buzz and excitement for the course.
- Give you the moral high-ground with learners and leaders who may blame you for their failure to read, listen to, or watch what you send them.

To accomplish these objectives, it is incumbent on you to leverage every communication channel at your disposal to connect with your learners before, during, and after training.

Leverage Multiple Communication Channels

Never, ever assume that people are reading and consuming what you send them.

You can put money on the fact that learners and leaders will not read the emails that you send them about the virtual training delivery. There are a number of reasons for this, including overwhelmed inboxes, competing priorities, spam filters, and passive resistance when learners see no value in the training or they don't wish to attend.

Attention spans have contracted. The modern world moves at light speed. Information overload is a state of being for most people. Attention is currency and, make no mistake, you are in a pitched battle for your learners' attention.

In addition, with the many ways we communicate in the modern world, people tend to gravitate toward preferred channels. If you are not communicating on that channel, the people who do may miss your message.

Leveraging as many channels as possible improves your probability of gaining attention. With attention, you can win mindshare. When you win learner mindshare, you gain the ability to accomplish your training mission.

Effective communication requires a mindset shift. For many trainers, this means getting out of your communication comfort zone. You'll need to get comfortable communicating via email, LMS, direct messaging, web chat, social media, video, phone—even smoke signals, if that's what it takes.

First, you must overcome your fear that when you overcommunicate, people will push back. Some people will, but that doesn't matter. What matters is eliminating confusion and getting participants into your virtual classroom, on time, and ready to learn.

Next, you'll need to master and become adept at communicating through a complex web of interconnected communication channels—synchronous and asynchronous—often at the same time. *Interconnected* is the key word. There isn't one best way. In today's world, communication channels are not siloed. When you leverage multiple communication channels, you are more likely to meet learners where they are and get your message across.

Communicating Virtual Classroom Access

The most common virtual training fail occurs when learners try to access the live virtual classroom on your videoconferencing platform. It is the one area that causes the most confusion for learners. Therefore, clearly communicating this information is your first and most important priority.

Make Access Information Easy to Find

Post the access information in a place that is easy for learners to find. If, like us, you leverage your LMS to run your virtual courses, start with clearly posting the information within the course structure there. If you don't run your virtual trainings on your LMS, ensure that the information is posted in a place where learners may easily access it like:

- Internal groups (think Slack or Teams)
- Private social media groups
- Syllabus page on your company intranet

Double-Check Access Information

When you are running multiple courses, it's super easy to make a mistake when posting or sending the virtual classroom information. Check it once, check it twice, check it three times before you post and send. At our company, we always have a third party do the final check. It's that important.

Communicate Early and Often

Send the virtual classroom information (video conference link and login) to learners multiple times through multiple channels. I've found that sending it daily for an entire week prior to the start of the course, resolves 99.9 percent of issues with confused learners who can't log in.

Calendar Invitations

When it makes sense, send a calendar invite that includes the virtual classroom information or a link back to the virtual classroom information. We typically include a link to the information page on our LMS because we want learners to get used to going to the course in the LMS for information rather than relying on email.

It helps to send a formal calendar invite that includes all recurring sessions in the course. This gets the virtual training sessions on learners' calendars. It also helps you gauge who has accepted the meeting and who has not so that you can follow up.

To avoid confusing learners, send a proper meeting invite that clearly indicates how learners should access the virtual classroom. Avoid taking the lazy route and just sending the generic invitation produced by your videoconferencing platform (Figure 23.1). Instead, customize the invitation and remove all superfluous information (Figure 23.2).

Jeb Blount is inviting you to a scheduled Zoom meeting.
Topic: Virtual Training
Time: May 3, 2022 010:00 AM Eastern Time (US and Canada)
Join Zoom Meeting
https://zoom.us/j/94348310511
Meeting ID: 943 4831 0511
One tap mobile
+13017158592,,94348310511# US (Germantown)
+13126266799,,94348310511# US (Chicago)
Dial by your location
    +1 301 715 8592 US (Germantown)
    +1 312 626 6799 US (Chicago)
    +1 646 558 8656 US (New York)
    +1 253 215 8782 US (Tacoma)
    +1 346 248 7799 US (Houston)
    +1 669 900 6833 US (San Jose)
Meeting ID: 943 4831 0511
Find your local number: https://zoom.us/u/aKGmKJ5xc
Join by SIP
94348310511@zoomcrc.com
Join by H.323
162.255.37.11 (US West)
162.255.36.11 (US East)
115.114.131.7 (India Mumbai)
115.114.115.7 (India Hyderabad)
213.19.144.110 (EMEA)
103.122.166.55 (Australia)
209.9.211.110 (Hong Kong China)
64.211.144.160 (Brazil)
69.174.57.160 (Canada)
207.226.132.110 (Japan)
Meeting ID: 943 4831 0511

Figure 23.1 The wrong way to invite learners to the virtual classroom. Avoid using the generic invitation produced by your video conferencing platform.

Virtual Training: Sales Prospecting Skills Training |
Four Sessions
Topic: Virtual Selling Skills Training for AMCO Sales Team
Dates: Tuesdays: May 3, 10, 17, 24
Time: 10:00 AM – 12:00 AM Eastern Time (120 Minutes)
Platform: Zoom
Required: Video On
Virtual Classroom Link to Join: https://zoom.us/j/
94348310511
Meeting ID: 943 4831 0511

**Figure 23.2 The right way to invite learners to the
virtual classroom. Use a customized invitation that
contains all the information they need—and nothing else.**

Pre-course Assignments and Creating Buzz

The three most important words in virtual training are engagement, engagement, and engagement. Getting learners engaged should begin long before the first session. I recommend initiating communication two full weeks prior to the first session.

Leverage pre-course communication to:

- Encourage learners to log in to the LMS.
- Introduce yourself (a best practice is to make a personalized video).
- Encourage learners to complete pre-course assignments.
- Assign self-paced e-learning elements.
- Compel learners to get engaged with pre-assessments, dynamic polls, and group discussions.
- Walk learners through the syllabus, expectations, and class rules.
- Teach them how to use the videoconferencing platform, discussion groups, virtual whiteboard, and core elements of the LMS.
- Create buzz.

Since you are working with adult learners, your primary objective is to get them excited about the training and get them connected to why the training is relevant to them. Pre-course buzz should answer the learners' most pressing question: "What's in it for me?"

We love to use video trailers that highlight key elements of the training and introduce the trainer. We also leverage fun memes, motivational quotes, and success stories to create excitement. Creating buzz requires you to both think like a marketer and have fun with it.

We've found through experience that, when we get learners involved and excited during the pre-course period, they are far more engaged and ready to learn when the course begins. It also helps us zero in on learners that are not engaging early so that we can reach out to them individually and pull them in.

Inter-Class Communication

Because you are dealing with adult learners and because there are usually days or weeks separating the live virtual sessions, it is important that you maintain a strong connection with your learners. Otherwise, once they go back to their daily routine, they forget about the course and you.

Communicating between VILT sessions should primarily be focused on:

- Reinforcing learning with recaps of key points (our trainers like to send video recaps)
- Links to the session replay video and session whiteboard image or PDF
- Reminders to complete homework and assignments
- Comments/praise for homework completions
- Prompts to engage in discussion groups
- Links to self-paced e-learning elements and micro-learning

- Links to other resources
- Previews of the next session

When you are juggling lots of training deliveries and a full schedule of commitments, it can be easy to forget to communicate to your learners between classes. To stay on track, create a communication checklist and block 30–60 minutes on your calendar each morning and afternoon for learner communication.

Finally, you should never, ever assume that learners have saved the access information for your virtual classroom (videoconferencing platform) or have session dates logged into their calendar. Therefore, you should send out reminders prior to each session—the day before and the morning of—that include the session time and platform access information. This simple communication removes the excuse: "I didn't know it was today."

Post-Class Communication

Our ultimate mission as trainers is to make a positive impact on the people we train and help them learn, grow, develop, stretch, and win. To fulfill this mission and affect long-term behavior change, the training must stick. This is why effective trainers leverage an ongoing 60- to 90-day communication plan following the conclusion of the training.

Your post-class communication plan should systematically and methodically anchor the learning with layered micro-learning, post-training assessments, prompts, group discussion boards, and one-to-one coaching when it makes sense.

For example, following my courses, I give learners access to special number that allows them to text me with questions and for help when they get stuck. This, along with a post-training survey, keeps me connected with my students and helps me become aware of any gaps in my training delivery or curriculum that I need to fill.

One of the challenges with VILT communication is that it often seems one way. It can feel like that old James Taylor song: You send long letters and get back postcards. It most cases, you get no response at all. For this reason, consistent communication and working your communication plan requires a bit of faith that you are making an impact. And you are. The more you communicate, the better the experience for your learners and the more they will be engaged—even if they don't always acknowledge your efforts.

Leveraging Video Messaging Along the Learning Journey

We consume video online at an ever-accelerating pace. Video accounts for 75 percent of internet traffic and is projected to rise to 82 percent in the near future.[1]

As a training and communication tool, video has moved from cutting edge to essential. Likewise, video is a powerful way for you to communicate with participants before, during, and following your course.

What I love most about video messaging is its versatility. Video messaging may be leveraged throughout the entirety of the learning journey. You've learned that your training participants emotional experience while working with you is the most consistent predictor of outcome of any other variable. At every stage of the course, video messaging, used well, helps you deliver a positive learning experience.

Leverage video messaging for:

- Pre-class welcome messages
- Coaching for individual learners
- Intra-class reminders and assignment prompts
- Post-session review and summaries
- Follow-up on homework assignments
- Personalized feedback and praise

Shooting Video Messages Is Wickedly Easy

For all of the reasons we've already discussed, the first step to lever-aging video messaging is getting past your aversion to being on camera. Let me assure you that the more video messages you create, the easier it will get.

Stop thinking about it and push record. Let go of your perfectionism. Most of these videos will be viewed once. They don't need to be absolutely perfect. So, loosen up and have fun with it.

Video messages should be short. Thirty to 120 seconds is optimal. You want your video messages to be authentic and feel spontaneous. This doesn't mean that you should just wing it. It doesn't mean that you should be sloppy. You need to be thoughtful about your message and process.

It *does* mean that elaborate video production is unnecessary. This makes shooting video messages easy because you can shoot them anywhere, anytime, with almost any backdrop. Even so, always look behind you before you shoot, and always check what's behind you on video before you push send. While just about any back-drop is acceptable for video messages, it is important that you avoid backdrops that may damage your personal brand or be offensive.

The beautiful thing about shooting video messages is that you have an excellent camera for this in your pocket right now. Just whip out that smartphone and start shooting. Likewise, you can simply turn on your webcam and record a video message from your training studio. It really is that easy.

Framing is still important. Make sure your torso is visible, that you are making eye contact, that the vertical and horizontal axis lines are symmetrical. If you are shooting with your phone, use a tripod that allows you to step back from the camera. (See Chapter 15 to refresh yourself on the basics of framing.)

If I am with someone, I get that person to hold my phone and shoot the video for me. While shooting, I ask them to very slowly and smoothly move the camera horizontally back and forth. This slight movement adds dimension to my video, which grabs attention. It is a form of *pattern painting*. If you look closely, you'll notice similar movements in movies and TV shows.

Lights

The camera needs light to capture a good picture. Most spaces indoors and outdoors will have enough light for good video messaging. Webcams, though, often require supplemental lighting such as an LED ring light for a good picture.

Always avoid shooting with bright windows or the sun behind you because you'll end up in "witness protection." Also avoid recording with bright windows or the sun directly in front of you, because if the light is too bright, it will wash you out.

Audio

For video messages, the microphone on your phone or webcam will do the trick. Certainly, if you have a setup with a professional microphone, you should use it, but it's not necessary for these types of short-and-sweet messages.

The good news is that the microphone on your camera is so good that it will isolate your voice against background noise even in busy offices, airports, and streets. You just want to avoid really loud noises, like a car honking, that can distract from your message. And always, always, always avoid rooms that generate big echoes.

Editing

The basics of editing video messages include these steps:

- Clip the beginning and end to remove the typical fumbling around as you turn record on or off.
- Add graphic overlays that support your training message or even your company logo to the lower right-hand corner.

- Cut out long pauses and mistakes.
- Add captions. This can take a few minutes, but if you are good enough to do it quickly, it will get more of your messages viewed because your learner won't need to turn their sound on to "hear" your message.

Your phone probably came with a simple editing tool and you can find any number of mobile and desktop apps that make it easy to quickly edit your video messages easy. With editing, the more you practice and get a workflow down, the faster you'll get. I've included a list of video editing apps at https://www.salesgravy.com/vt. Remember to use code VTB2021X when you check out to gain free access to these resources.

Sending Video Messages

There are multiple options for sending video messages, including email, text, and direct messaging. You may simply upload your message to the LMS and distribute it from there. Or, set up a free Vidyard, Loom, Vimeo, or YouTube account and send a private link in an email, text, or direct message.

Personalized Video Messages

Academic studies prove that people love and crave content that is personalized for them.[2] But you already know this because you are human, and you do, too. The most insatiable human need and craving is to feel important, appreciated, significant. We all want to know that we matter.

A video that was made *just for you*, makes you feel this way. Which is one of the key reasons why personalized videos are such a powerful and compelling communication channel.

Because the need for significance is so insatiable, when you make a learner feel important you give them the greatest gift that you can give another person. The beautiful thing about gifts is, when you give one, it compels the other person to *feel* the need to reciprocate.

Robert B. Cialdini, author of *Influence*, says, "One of the most potent of the weapons of influence around us is the rule for reciprocation. The rule says that we should try to repay, in kind, what another person has provided us."[3] This feeling of obligation, the need to reciprocate, is baked deep into human psychology.

In layman's terms, the law of reciprocity simply explains that when you give a learner a gift—like a personalized video message, praise, or individual attention—it triggers a subconscious feeling of obligation. This feeling increases the probability that they will engage, participate, learn, and give you a high rating on post-training surveys.

24 | The Fine Art of Engagement

Lights, camera, action! You and your students enter the virtual classroom. This is the moment of truth, where the rubber meets the road with virtual training. This is where everything comes together.

In previous chapters, you learned about how production quality and technology improve the learner experience. We've discussed the essentials of design, planning, communication, setting rules, and controlling your classroom.

Yet, for all the technology, production, and equipment, that pivotal moment when you connect with your learners, face to face on-screen is where the real magic happens. Before we dive into the art of engaging learners in the virtual classroom, let's take a moment to reflect on what we've learned so far:

- With virtual training, you are always on stage and you must be prepared.

- Good enough is not good enough.
- The way virtual training is delivered and how it makes learners feel is what matters most.
- When the virtual learning experience is emotionally positive, participants will be more engaged, and learning will stick.
- When learners are engaged and participating, you are more fulfilled and feel that you made an impact.
- Traditionally, most virtual training has been an awful experience because it is not engaging.

The real secret to gaining widespread acceptance of virtual training is delivering an exceptional virtual learning experience. This begins and ends with learner engagement—and that lies at the intersection of technology and human connection.

When it comes to engagement, the jump to VILT brings new challenges and considerations—it also takes some getting used to. Achieving learner engagement can seem like an overwhelming concept, but if you break it down into the key components, it becomes much more manageable.

Win Learners Over

Although virtual training is made possible by technology, it is still a uniquely human endeavor. Training and learning are woven into the imperfect fabric of human emotion.

The ability to manage technology and leverage virtual communication skills allows us to create the highest level of virtual learning experience. This is what separates average trainers from the true professionals.

Viet Thanh Nguyen is a college professor and novelist who believes in the value of virtual instruction. He says that although the virtual classroom may have less human warmth, there is often more human connection. These connections facilitate an environment in which students have an enthusiastic willingness to participate, collaborate, and engage.[1]

One of the challenges with remote instruction is that the distance deludes trainers into believing that it is OK to shortchange human connections. The truth is that in virtual training, those connections are even more important. They may be challenging to build, but when they're supported, they can result in deep, meaningful learning experiences.

Make Learners Feel Important

The most insatiable human desire, our deepest craving, is to feel significant, valued, and appreciated. The key to connecting and winning learners over is, therefore, extremely simple: *make them feel important.*

In the physical classroom, we always start a course by giving each participant an opportunity to introduce themselves. We ask them to give us a short career history, share their challenges and expectations for the course, and tell us something unique or interesting about themselves. It's a powerful way to begin training because it gets learners involved early, gives them the opportunity to talk about themselves, and allows the trainer to quickly build rapport with them.

This same process is vitally important in the virtual classroom. We begin with a pre-course discussion board for the learners and trainers to connect and introduce themselves via text or video. Then, in the virtual classroom, we ask learners to tell their story. We ask them to:

- Give a short history of themselves.
- Tell us why they chose their current job role.
- Share something unique about themselves.

Our trainers then use this information as they advance through the course to engage participants, personalize the experience, and shape the course content around their learners.

Build Learner Profiles

Our most effective, respected, and loved trainers are masters at calling learners by name and remembering key details about them. They win learners over by making each learner feel as if the training was built just for them.

But engaging and connecting with learners at this level can be challenging when you are teaching multiple courses and working with dozens and sometimes hundreds of participants. This is exactly why conscientious trainers build individual learner profiles.

These profiles can be built on paper, in your CRM, talent management system, or in your LMS. On these profiles, instructors record key information about the participants. They log notes about each learner's engagement, questions they are asking, examples they give, and so on. This information is then leveraged to encourage engagement and strengthen connections.

Logging information on learner profiles is a powerful way to stand out as a trainer and win learners over. It only requires intention, discipline, and a system for managing the information you collect.

Effective Listening

The real secret to engaging learners though is not what you say; it's what you hear.

Your ability to tune in, turn on, and truly listen to your learners is what makes you an engaging trainer. You must not only hear what they say, but you must also become adept at reading between the lines and accurately interpreting what they are not saying.

Effective listening is the ability to actively understand information expressed by your learners while causing them to feel that you are paying attention, interested, and care. It is listening with the intent to understand rather than a desire to respond.

No single skill is more important for a trainer in the virtual classroom than effective listening. It's the key to developing deep emotional connections and most importantly flexing to the unique needs of each learning cohort and individual participant. Effective listening helps you tailor and shape each training delivery around your learners.

Despite this, listening is often the weakest part of virtual training. The sad fact is that in most virtual classrooms, trainers talk and talk and talk, boring learners to death.

The Person Who Is Listening Is Always in Control

Think about a time when you were trying to explain something to another person. Recall the moment, right in the middle of your story, that the other person held up a hand and said, "Stop! Could you just get to the point?"

Consider how that made you feel. Were you hurt? Did you feel unappreciated, angry, or enraged? Were you left with the feeling that the other person didn't understand you?

How about the time you were trying to have a conversation with a friend, and they kept looking down at their phone at incoming text messages? Did you want to rip the phone from their hand and smash it on the floor?

Have you ever been excited to tell your significant other about your day? You talked, but the other person was not paying attention because he or she was watching TV, playing a video game, or typing away on a computer?

"You're not even listening to me!" you complained in disgust. "I don't know why I even bother."

As your significant other replied with a "Huh?" while barely averting attention from the screen, did you feel more emotionally connected or in love in that moment? I doubt it. You know the truth, and so do I. When people don't listen to you, it makes you feel small, unappreciated, and unimportant.

Some trainers fail to listen because they are so nervous about being on camera or working with tech. Others are insecure and self-conscious about engaging with other people in a virtual environment.

Still others falsely believe that to be in control of the virtual classroom, they must be doing all of the talking. They forget a basic tenet of human communication: *The person who is listening, is always in control.*

In person, there are far more visual cues that signal when you need to shut up, ask a question, and give your learners an opportunity to express themselves. Because of the limitations on communication in the virtual classroom—including poor connections, microphones, and poor participant video frames—listening requires much more focus and patience than in a physical classroom. It requires your discipline to be present and in the moment.

This is one of the key reasons why talking rather than listening becomes the default for many trainers. It's just easier.

Active Listening

Effective listening in the virtual classroom begins with active listening. This is a set of behaviors that provide tangible proof that you are paying attention and engaged.

Active listening rewards learners for talking and expressing themselves. The more that learners talk, the more they remain engaged, and the more dynamic the virtual classroom. Active listening includes these behaviors:

- Acknowledge that you are listening. Look directly at the camera and make eye contact.
- Use affirmative body language and facial expressions to demonstrate that you are listening. Smile. Lean forward toward the camera and nod your head.
- Summarize and restate what the learner said. This not only tells them you are listening but aids understanding.
- Ask relevant follow-up questions that build on the conversation. This validates that you are paying attention and encourages learners to open up and continue to actively participate.
- Use supporting phrases like "Yes, I see," "That makes sense."

Deep Listening

Learners, however, communicate with far more than words. To truly hear them, you must listen with all your senses—eyes, ears, and intuition. This is called *deep listening*.

Opening your senses to become aware of the entire message affords you the opportunity to analyze the emotional nuances within your virtual classroom. As you listen:

- Be observant and tune in.
- Pay attention to the tone, timbre, and pace of your learners' voices.
- Be aware of body language and micro-expressions.
- Focus on the meaning behind the words they are using.
- Be alert for emotional cues—both verbal and nonverbal.

Since people tend to communicate in stories, listen deeply to pick up unsaid feelings and emotions. As you perceive emotional importance, ask relevant follow-up questions to pull information out of the learner and keep them engaged. For example, "That sounds pretty important. Tell me more?"

Pause Before You Speak to Avoid Awkwardness

One sure way to kill conversation and engagement and create the awkward, uncomfortable pauses that so often plague virtual classrooms is to blurt out your next question or statement and talk over a learner before they have finished speaking.

With both parties talking over each other, communication grinds to a halt. It also becomes transparent that you are not listening with the intent to understand, but rather, to formulate the next thing you plan to say.

In the virtual classroom, learn to pause before speaking. Pausing leaves room for others to finish speaking and prevents you from cutting them off, making the conversation more natural. When you feel that the other person has finished speaking, pause and count to three. This solves for both the inevitable glitches and delays inherent in live stream communication *and* allows you to fully digest what you have heard, before responding.

When your learner slows down in an attempt to gather their thoughts or find a way to fully express their feelings or an idea, it is easy to become impatient, jump in, and finish the sentence for them. More often than not, when you do this, you end up way off base because you had no idea what they were actually thinking. This uninvited interruption can create frustration and worse, shut the learner down (especially the shy mouse).

Learn to listen without jumping to conclusions or making snap judgments. Remember that your learners use language to represent their thoughts and feelings. Don't assume that you know what those thoughts and feeling are and finish their sentences.

When you are unclear about what your learner is saying, or you don't understand something they are trying to express, you'll want to clarify. In this moment, it is easy to make the mistake of interrupting them mid-sentence with a question.

Don't do this. Instead, wait until they pause, and then ask your clarifying question. Well-timed clarifying questions make learners feel important and reward engagement. They demonstrate that you care, are listening, and are interested in understanding them.

Pattern Painting

In simplest terms, your brain is like a Russian nesting doll.

- **The big doll on the outside is the neocortex.** This is your gray matter, your rational brain that helps you reason, make decisions, and think.
- **The middle doll is the limbic system.** This is your brain's emotional center.
- **The smallest doll, is your brain stem and cerebellum.** This part of the brain manages your sympathetic nervous system and all the little (but still important) things, like breathing, so you can concentrate on what's most important.

All three parts of the brain are connected, either directly or indirectly, to the amygdala, a small structure housed in the limbic system. The amygdala helps your brain connect experiences with emotions, which triggers motivation and helps determine what's worth focusing on and what's not. This allows your brain to avoid wasting precious cognitive resources on things that don't matter.

To do this instantly, the amygdala relies on patterns. It ignores boring patterns, which are made by things you've encountered before and didn't have much emotional reaction to. It also focuses on new experiences and environmental disruptions, including anything different, out of place, unexpected, bright, shiny, sexy, new, or threatening.

Pattern recognition provides us with a simple cognitive shortcut to help us quickly become alert to anything new and unexpected. It is a key survival mechanism. Pattern disrupters can be threats or opportunities, so it makes sense to pay attention to them.

In other words, when things are moving and changing in your environment, your brain is activated, and you are paying attention. For learners, to avoid wasting cognitive resources, the amygdala acts as a gate to their neocortex, letting in information that it deems important and blocking that which it deems boring and unimportant.

Therefore, if you are boring, you become a dull pattern. Participants will quit paying attention and stop learning. You are not interesting. You are not memorable. Your learners' amygdala closes the gate. They turn you off.

Painting this boring gray pattern with bright colors changes everything. When you disrupt expectations during virtual training sessions, you pull learners toward you and grab their attention. The real secret to painting these patterns and grabbing attention is:

- Using good production that keeps the screen changing.
- Maintaining momentum.
- Making your virtual classroom interactive and fun.
- Bringing the content to life with stories and examples.

When participants are doing, they are engaged, and when they are engaged, they are learning, and when they are learning, they are happy.

Fostering Discussion

The biggest complaints from learners about virtual training concern lack of engagement between the instructor and learners, uncomfortable silence, and awkward pauses. Your effectiveness with fostering and engaging in discussion allows you to solve for these problems to deliver a better virtual learning experience.

From the get-go you want to create a relaxed environment that makes it easy and safe for learners to ask questions, push back, and engage in discussions—just like in a physical classroom.

A best practice is to begin the course with a conversation about how to interact in a virtual environment. Acknowledge that it is hard to know when it is ok to speak, that you'll sometimes talk over each other, and that interrupting to ask questions is encouraged.

Teach learners how to interrupt. In my classrooms, I encourage learners to just blurt it out or raise their hand. Of course, you may prefer chat or some other means of getting your attention. What is most important is giving learners a way to stop you and engage in a discussion.

Pausing to check in with learners is crucial when teaching in the virtual classroom because you won't have the same visual cues that you would in person. Checking in keeps you connected to your learners, encourages them to interact, gives you feedback, and brings potential concerns to the surface.

Pause after each slide or after important points within a slide to check participant temperatures.

"Does that make sense?"

"May I answer any questions about that?"

"How is my pace? Am I moving too fast or too slow?"

Sometimes these questions will be rhetorical, especially when you're establishing a flow so learners know that they can ask questions after each slide. You'll pause, ask the question, check learner faces on your screen, and keep moving. At times, especially with the last question, I'll ask for a thumbs up or thumbs down, which learners will readily give.

Ask Questions Purposefully

What's important to understand about engaging learners in discussions is whenever you ask a general question to the group like: "Does anyone have any questions about that that?" You will be met with awkward silence. You won't get a response.

Therefore, when you want a response and to avoid uncomfortable and awkward pauses, call learners by name. The most effective technique for getting learners to engage in discussions is to pose the question to them directly.

> *"Bob, you said during the last breakout on customer service challenges that this was an issue for you. How do you feel this technique will work in the field?"*
>
> *"Emily, does this answer your question about the way we handle service issues with angry customers?"*
>
> *"Praveen, what does this mean to you?"*
>
> *"Maria, does this make sense?"*

Use random patterns when calling on learners so that they never know when their name will come up. This will force them to remain alert and engaged. The good news is that the more learners interact in discussions, the more comfortable they'll feel naturally interrupting you.

"Everyone Unmute"

Back to those awkward pauses. Another cause for awkward pauses is the time it takes for the learner to unmute themselves to answer your question. Likewise, there are the learners who forget to unmute and have to be told to unmute. This can be uncomfortable and it takes up time.

When I want to have a more fluid conversation about an especially important issue and I want to get more learners involved in the conversations without this friction I'll say: "OK, I want everyone to unmute so that we can have a rapid-fire, free-flowing conversation."

Once everyone is off mute, I begin throwing questions at them. The discussion moves at a much faster pace and it becomes easier to get people talking.

Turn Bullet Points into Conversation

To be engaging, virtual training must be a conversation, not a presentation. No one wants to listen to you read bullet points.

When you are presenting information or concepts from a bullet-pointed slide, one of the easiest and most effective ways to test knowledge and get learners engaged is to turn those bullet points into conversation topics.

You might read the point and then ask, "Manny, what does this mean?" or you might say, "Carrie, read the first bullet point on this slide and tell us what it means."

Do Not Answer Your Own Questions

The silence, after you pose a question, can be incredibly uncomfortable and make you feel deeply insecure. So instead of waiting, you jump in, fill the vacuum and give the learner the answer. This is a huge mistake!

Human behavior is basic and predictable. Any behavior that gets positive reinforcement tends to repeat and become more frequent. Any behavior that receives a negative reinforcement tends to decrease in frequency.

When you answer your own questions, you reward your learners' silence and teach them that if they freeze you out, you'll cave and do their work for them. The more they respond with silence, the more you feel insecure and answer your own questions.

Soon, your training delivery isn't much more than a broadcast of you reading bullet points while your learners watch cat videos on YouTube as you drone on.

The first rule of virtual classroom engagement is: *Never answer your own questions.*

When you ask a question in a virtual classroom, you'll usually be met with silence. This is because microphones are on mute and each learner is waiting for the other participants to answer.

The most challenging technique for trainers to master in the virtual classroom is learning how to pose a question to the group or an individual and then *shut up.*

The awkward silence after you ask a question can feel unbearable—like an eternity. In this moment of weakness, you start talking, and talking, and talking. Your brain deluded you into believing that you are doing the right thing, but you are not. Talking isn't engaging.

After you ask a question, *shut up!* Despite the alarm bells going off in your adrenaline-soaked mind, despite your pounding heart, sweaty palms, and fear, you must bite your tongue, sit on your hands, and allow your learners to answer.

And they will, because the silence is unbearable to them, too. If you just wait patiently, one of the learners will speak up. When they do, praise them and provide positive feedback. This, in turn, teaches participants that answering and engaging gets rewarded.

Of course, there are times when learners just stare back at you because they don't understand. Perhaps it was how you structured the question; perhaps they are not connecting the dots. In situations like this, rather than breaking the rule and answering your own question:

- Restate the question or ask it in a different way.
- Give them an analogy and then ask the question again.
- Tell a story and ask the question again.
- Smile and point to (or mention) the slide on the screen that contains the answer and say: "Folks, this is an open-book test."

There will be a few instances when you ask a difficult question of learners and are met with blank stares. When you can tell by reading their faces that they truly don't have the answer, only then should you answer your own question and teach them the answer.

Interactivity

We've all been in trainings where the instructor delivers a lecture, peppered with a few questions and answers. It's the fastest way to drain your participants' energy and doom them to boredom. Engagement relies on interactivity. This is even more important in virtual training. There are a number of techniques—outlined in this section—you should use to encourage interactivity and give learners a chance to shape their experience. This not only creates a more enjoyable experience but also helps them reinforce their own learning.

Breakouts

During training sessions, most of the learning occurs in the breakout exercises. This is exactly why we include at least two breakout sessions for every hour of virtual training.

Breakout sessions allow learners to work through problems and mental roadblocks, discuss issues, and gain insight and best practices from each other.

Learners love these small-group breakouts, and most video conferencing platforms make facilitating breakouts easy and seamless.

To avoid awkward pauses that slow momentum, make sure you are adept at moving learners into breakouts. It helps to set up your breakout groups in advance or at the beginning of class, when learners first come into the virtual classroom. To ensure smooth transitions into virtual breakout sessions, provide clear instructions, including the expected deliverables and timing.

A big mistake that I've noticed with trainers is using the breakout session as an opportunity to take a break. This is bad behavior that causes you to miss out on coaching opportunities and breakout discussions. It also sends the message that the breakouts are not important to you.

During breakouts, cycle through each room so that you are present in each group to answer questions and give feedback. I'll typically cycle through the breakout groups, continuously spending two minutes with each group before moving to the next.

Being in the groups allows me to keep my fingers on the pulse of my learners, gain insight into what they are thinking, and bring that insight back to the larger group to foster more impactful conversations.

Whiteboard

You should always have a whiteboard visible on your virtual training set—just as you might have in the physical classroom.

During discussions, and for illustrating points, diagrams, and capturing ideas, there is no better tool than a whiteboard. When you are writing on the whiteboard, learners lean in and pay attention, especially when you are writing down *their* idea or point.

Digital whiteboards or smart boards (though expensive) are even better because they allow learners to both collaborate with you and view the whiteboard in real time on their own device.

We leverage smart boards during breakout sessions. We give each breakout group a page on the board to capture their notes. It makes reporting out smoother and allows everyone to see and learn from each group's work. Following each session, we create a PDF of all the notes on the smart board and forward them to our learners.

Role-Play

Practicing new skills via role-play is one of the most effective ways to anchor knowledge and keep learners actively engaged.

Role-plays effectively turn your virtual training into a reality TV show, making it very hard for learners to tune out.

As the trainer, you must be comfortable role-playing every concept you are teaching. You gain respect and credibility when you demonstrate skills via role-play. And, when you are demonstrating, learners pay attention.

A best practice for kicking off role-play sessions is to choose two learners to demonstrate for the entire group. Spotlight the two learners so that their video frames are side-by-side on-screen. Have them role-play and then give them feedback and coaching.

Once you've demonstrated for everyone, break the learners into groups of two to three and send them into breakout rooms to role-play on their own. Be sure that you are cycling through the breakout rooms and observing.

Polls, Surveys, and Quizzes

Most video conferencing platforms allow you to create polls, surveys, and quizzes that you can give to learners in real time. The key to leveraging these interactive elements is planning in advance so that you launch them smoothly, without awkward pauses. Used wisely, these interactive tools can bring an element of fun to the classroom and keep learners engaged and on their toes.

Have Fun

Bringing interactive games, competitions, and fun activities to the virtual classroom is an excellent way to lower emotional walls, paint patterns, and keep learners engaged. All it takes to have fun is your imagination, intention, and a little bit of planning.

For example, Gina Trimarco, one of our master trainers, runs an activity while teaching observation skills in which everyone turns off their video feed and makes a change to their environment. Then when the camera's come back on, learners must identify what has changed in each frame. We get the highest survey scores and best feedback from this activity.

Pacing

Pacing is another important factor in learner engagement. Breaks and slide pacing are two of the biggest considerations to help you ensure your learners will be able to stay with you.

Take a Break

When virtual sessions stretch beyond 120 minutes, schedule breaks to allow you and your participants to disconnect for a moment and refresh. Well-timed breaks also allow learners to deal with issues in their environment and on the job that could potentially distract them.

Do Not Rush Your Slides

It is important to maintain momentum in the virtual classroom. When things are moving, learners are paying attention. However, you must not move too fast or too slow.

Your pace and speed should give participants the time they need to fully digest your key points without lingering too long on a slide or shortchanging your learners by moving too fast.

One of the biggest turn-offs for learners is a trainer rushing through slides at the end of a training session just to get them in. It is disconcerting to learners, who feel short-changed by this bad behavior, and you'll see their complaints show up in post-course surveys.

Everything in the virtual classroom tends to take longer. This is why lesson planning is so important. When you know the content and you have your timing down for each lesson, it's much easier to remain on track. But even with the best planning, you may run out of time. A top dog may get you off track, discussion and breakouts might take longer than expected, or technical snags can slow things down. In these situations, you may run out of time.

When you find yourself in these situations, *do not rush your slides*. Instead, take a breath and make one of three choices.

- Skip some of the less important content and focus on the lessons that matter most.
- Save the content for the next session.
- Add a make-up session.

Bring Content to Life

Because virtual instructor-led training is such a demanding training modality, the ultimate success of the learning experience rests on your ability to bring the content and curriculum to life. The good news is that the attributes and communication skills that allow you to deliver a legendary learning experience in the physical classroom serve you just as well in the virtual classroom.

However, the natural limitations of the virtual classroom require you to take your communication skills to the next level. To be effective, you need to be authentic, comfortable, confident, enthusiastic, approachable, and intuitive. Learners expect and demand authentic, natural human interaction. When you sound stiff, scripted, fake, arrogant, or patronizing, it turns them off.

Use a friendly tone with a smile in your voice and on your face. Lean in when you are making an important point. Lean out and pause when you want to allow some space for introspection. Speak with normal inflection at a relaxed pace with appropriate voice modulation and pause for or place emotional emphasis on the right words and phrases.

What you say matters. *How* you say it matters more. While a learner's neocortex (rational brain) is busy interpreting your words, the emotional center of their brain is listening closely to your tone, timbre, pace, and inflection for hidden meaning.

Learners are looking for congruency between what they hear and see. The way we say it at Sales Gravy is "making sure your video and audio match."

Anybody can stand there and read bullet points. Master trainers, however, connect the dots with learners through stories. They bring the content to life and demonstrate authenticity through analogies, examples, and personal stories.

When you leverage stories in the classroom, you grab and hold attention. Good story tellers have a flair for the dramatic. They draw their audience in with animated delivery and visualization. They weave in humor, pause for effect, speed up, slow down, make stories fun, and have fun telling them.

The most impactful stories are personal stories, often of failure and triumph over adversity, that show your vulnerability and make you human. The more relatable and emotional the story, the more likely that your learners will act on what they have learned.[2]

Participants won't remember your bullet points, but they almost always remember your stories. Stories packed with emotional content connect you with your learners and result in better understanding and recall.[3]

We are more likely to remember the emotions we feel when listening to stories because the brain places more importance and more attention on things that are emotional. This is one of the key reasons that stories aid in learner retention.

As you present the content, your stories stimulate and activate your learners' brains.[4] Research demonstrates that the human brain loves stories. We are happier, more empathetic, more motivated, more engaged, and more willing to be collaborative following stories.

The left side of the brain is concerned with analysis, facts, and data—the bullet points. Whereas the right side of the brain is the center for creativity and the big picture. Impactful stories create real change—to mindset, beliefs, and skill set—by connecting the left and right side of the brain around new concepts and ideas. Stories, therefore, are integral to helping learners assimilate and actualize new skills.

The Curriculum Is Your Canvas

Training content and curriculum is much like the painter's canvas. The art of training is pulling the beauty from that canvas and conveying it to your learners.

The key is mastering the material and then making it your own. Though the curriculum is often fixed, the strokes of the brush and the colors you paint are your choices to make. All it takes is your imagination, enthusiasm, and bringing in a relevant mix of stories and examples that connect with your learners.

There is an oft-expressed maxim: *Learners will forget what you said, they'll forget what you did, but they will never forget how you made them feel.* As humans, we feel, then we think, then we learn.

Reflection

1. List some ideas you have for improving or enhancing the design of your virtual training course curriculum and media. How might you leverage the Chunk, Layer, Sequence technique to make learning stick?

   _____

   _____

   _____

   _____

2. Develop your virtual training classroom rules and a communication plan template:

   _____

   _____

   _____

   _____

3. Build a virtual training delivery check-list and pre-training planning routine.

_____

_____

_____

_____

4. What are some actions you can take immediately to gain more control of your virtual classroom?

_____

_____

_____

_____

5. What are some steps you might take to enhance and elevate your virtual training delivery?

_____

_____

_____

_____

Notes:

_____

_____

_____

_____

_____

Prologue

Kleon stared out of the window of his university dorm room. It was early spring in Aberdeen, Scotland. The students who lived in the UK had all been sent home, leaving Kleon alone on the now-deserted campus. With the global pandemic kicking into high gear across Europe, he was unable to get a flight or train ticket back to his home in Greece.

He was lonely and worried that he'd be stuck in quarantine for the next six months. It was a thought that he found unbearable. So, when he concocted an insane idea: he would ride his bike back home to Greece—an idea that, at first, he told himself was impossible. But, deeply homesick and desperate, he struck out on the "impossible" journey with only his bike, sleeping bag, tent, canned sardines, peanut butter, and some bread.

At the end of the first day as he sat in his tent, he was sore, tired, and questioning his boneheaded decision. The enormity of the trip he'd embarked on was overwhelming. Part of him wanted to go back to his dorm room and its soft bed, food, TV, and internet. But instead of succumbing to the mental and physical pain, he got back on his bike the next day and kept peddling. Over the following

weeks as he camped in fields and along roadsides, he focused on
his mission to get back to his family in Greece and used it as fuel
to stay motivated.

Forty-eight days later, after crossing through five countries and
2000 miles, Kleon finally made it home to his family.

Ready Learner One

Now and in the future, leading organizations will be seamlessly
blending multiple training modalities to deliver more training,
faster, with better outcomes. We'll also begin a steady shift from
2D video-based virtual training into teaching in 3D virtual reality
and augmented reality spaces. This next level of virtual training will
change everything.

At Sales Gravy, we are already running beta virtual-reality
instructor-led trainings (VRILT) for a select group of clients.
Though we have a long way to go before we take it to a larger
group, we've made massive progress over the past year building our
Virtual Reality Classrooms and developing our training delivery
skills in virtual reality spaces.

I'm totally bought in. The virtual reality classroom is beyond
anything you have ever experienced. It is so incredible and so game
changing that it is impossible to adequately describe the power and
depth of this technology in words. It's truly one of those things you
must see to believe.

VRILT combines the best of classroom-based ILT and
virtual ILT in one sleek package. It is 100 times better than video
conferencing—and that is not an exaggeration.

Though VRILT as a ubiquitous mainstream training modality
is years away, my objective with these early investments of time and
money in VR is to keep Sales Gravy and our master trainers on the
leading edge.

Lift the Chains of Limitations

I'm an admitted evangelist for virtual training. I'm also the person who said that most of our courses at Sales Gravy could never be taught effectively in a virtual classroom.

I remember being adamant that one of our most popular courses, called "Coaching Ultra-High Performance" (one of my favorites to teach), which was taught in a two-day classroom-based experience, would be impossible to deliver virtually. I've been wrong on all counts. Today, that coaching course is more impactful as a virtual learning experience than it ever was in the classroom.

It would be easy at this juncture to claim that in-person training is dead. That entirely self-serving buzz-worthy proclamation would shock you and grab your attention. Yet, it would be wrong. Classroom-based training will continue to be a key piece of the adult learning puzzle. There are facets of human communication that can never be duplicated in virtual training—2D or 3D.

Still, if we learned anything in 2020 it's that we must endeavor to open ourselves up to new possibilities for how we teach, learn, and think about how knowledge and skill transfer can be accomplished. We must be willing to step out of old comfort zones and stretch ourselves to change and innovate.

The trip from Aberdeen, Scotland, to Greece changed Kleon. He said that it taught him that he was capable of doing more than he ever thought was possible. "I improved as a person," he said. "I'm more confident in myself, I'm more confident in my abilities.

"When you set the bar really high and you attempt to reach a really ambitious goal, whether you achieve it or you don't, you will have improved," he said. "You will learn things about yourself and you will surprise yourself."

Kleon learned that when you pull away the chains of your own self-imposed limitations, you free yourself to see that almost anything is possible.

Notes

Chapter 1   Just Like That, Everything Changed

1 eLearn2grow, "62 eLearning Stats and Facts That You Need to Know," eLearn2grow, June 16, 2020, https://www.elearn2grow.com/2020/06/16/elearning-stats/.

2 Darrell Etherington, "LinkedIn to Buy Online Education Site Lynda.com for $1.5 Billion," *TechCrunch,* April 9, 2015, https://techcrunch.com/2015/04/09/linkedin-to-buy-online-education-site-lynda-com-for-1-5-billion/.

3 Cindy Huggett, "Is Your Organization Ready for the Future of Virtual Training?" *Training Industry Magazine,* November/December 2018, https://trainingindustry.com/magazine/nov-dec-2018/is-your-organization-ready-for-the-future-of-virtual-training/.

4 William Leonard, "So Why Did MOOCs Fail to Live Up to the Hype?" *University World News,* February 8, 2019, https://www.universityworldnews.com/post.php?story=20190207110446568.

Chapter 3   The Case for Virtual Training

1 Christopher Pappas, "Top 20 eLearning Statistics for 2019 You Need to Know," eLearning Industry.com, September 24, 2019, https://elearningindustry.com/top-elearning-statistics-2019.

2 Justin Reich and José A. Ruipérez-Valiente, "The MOOC Pivot," *Science,* January 11, 2019, https://science.sciencemag.org/content/363/6423/130.

3 The Editors of Encyclopaedia Britannica, "Social Learning," Encyclopaedia Britannica, September 13, 2019, https://www.britannica.com/science/social-learning.

4 Richard E. Mayer, *Multimedia Learning* (Cambridge University Press, 2009), 175–188.

5 Sally Caird and Robin Roy, "Sustainable Higher Education Systems," in *Encyclopaedia of Sustainability and Higher Education,* ed. Walter Leal Filho (Springer Nature: 2019), https://doi.org/10.1007/978-3-319-63951-2_261-1.

Chapter 6   Mission and Mindset for a Legendary Virtual Learning Experience

1 Whitney Seltman, "Understanding Vision Problems—the Basics," WebMD, February 7, 2020, https://www.webmd.com/eye-health/understanding-vision-problems-basics.

2 Elizabeth Huber, Kelly Chang, Ivan Alvarez, Aaron Hundle, and Ione Fine, "Early Blindness Shapes Cortical Representations of Frequency within Auditory Cortex," *Journal of Neuroscience* 39, no. 26 (June 26, 2019): 5143–5152, https://www.jneurosci.org/content/39/26/5143.

3 Lotfi B. Merabet and Alvaro Pascual-Leone, "Neural Reorganization Following Sensory Loss: The Opportunity of Change," *National Review of Neuroscience* 11, no. 1 (January 2010): 44–52, https://www.ncbi.nlm.nih.gov/pmc/articles/PMC3898172/.

4 Fraser W. Smith and Stephanie Rossit, "Identifying and Detecting Facial Expressions of Emotion in Peripheral Vision," *PLoS One* 13, no. 5 (May 30, 2018), https://doi.org/10.1371/journal.pone.0197160.

Chapter 7   Emotional Discipline

1 Elaine Hatfield, John T. Cacioppo, and Richard L. Rapson, *Emotional Contagion* (New York: Cambridge University Press, 1994).

2 Shirley Wang, "Contagious Behavior," *Observer*, February 2006, Association for Psychological Science, https://www.psychological science.org/observer/contagious-behavior.

3 Brene Brown, *The Power of Vulnerability*. Narrated by the author (Sounds True, 2012), audiobook.

Chapter 8   Rise Above Your Tech and Video Camera Phobia

1 Highfive and Zogby Analytics, "Wondering How to Look Good on Video? You're Not Alone," Highfive.com, accessed April 6, 2021, highfive.com/resources/infographics/how-to-look-good-on-video.

Chapter 10   The Brain on Virtual Training

1 Richard Culatta, "Cognitive Load Theory (John Sweller)," InstructionalDesign.org, 2015, www.instructionaldesign.org/theories/cognitive-load.html.

2 Lauren Geall, "Have You Got Zoom Fatigue? Why You're Finding Video Calls So Exhausting," *Stylist*, April 2020, www.stylist.co.uk/life/zoom-fatigue-video-call-virtual-drinks-exhaustion-tiring/376846.

3 Jena Lee, "A Neuropsychological Exploration of Zoom Fatigue," *Psychiatric Times*, November 17, 2020. https://www.psychiatric-times.com/view/psychological-exploration-zoom-fatigue.

4 Manyu Jiang, "The Reason Zoom Calls Drain Your Energy," BBC, April 22, 2020, www.bbc.com/worklife/article/20200421-why-zoom-video-chats-are-so-exhausting.

5 Katrin Schoenenberg, Alexander Raake, and Judith Koeppe, "Why Are You So Slow? Misattribution of Transmission Delay to Attributes of the Conversation Partner at the Far-End," *International Journal of Human-Computer Studies* 72, no. 5 (May 2014): 477–487. www.sciencedirect.com/science/article/abs/pii/S1071581914000287.

6 Cisco, "Cisco Annual Internet Report," March 9, 2020, https://www.cisco.com/c/en/us/solutions/collateral/executive-perspectives/annual-internet-report/white-paper-c11-741490.html.

Chapter 11 The Essentials of Highly Effective Virtual Training Production

1 Jena Lee, "A Neuropsychological Exploration of Zoom Fatigue," *Psychiatric Times*, November 17, 2020. https://www.psychiatric times.com/view/psychological-exploration-zoom-fatigue.

Chapter 14 Be Video Ready

1 Ti Kiisel, "You Are Judged by Your Appearance," *Forbes,* March 20, 2013, www.forbes.com/sites/tykiisel/2013/03/20/you-are-judged-by-your-appearance/#523930726d50.
2 Egan Jiminez, "In a Split Second, Clothes Make the Man More Competent in the Eyes of Others," EurekaAlert! Princeton University, Woodrow Wilson School of Public and International Affairs, December 9, 2019, www.eurekalert.org/pub_releases/2019-12/puww-ias120919.php.
3 Nasim Mansurov, "What Is Moiré and How It Can Ruin Your Photos," *Photography Life*, December 24, 2019, photographylife. com/what-is-moire.
4 Gauri Sardi-Joshi, "What You Wear Changes That Way You Think," Brain Fodder, accessed April 16, 2021, https://brainfodder.org/psychology-clothes-enclothed-cognition/.
5 Hannah Yasharoff, "Viral Reporter Returns to 'GMA' after 'Hilariously Mortifying' Video Appearance with No Pants," *USA Today,* April 28, 2020, www.usatoday.com/story/entertainment/tv/2020/04/28/quarantine-woes-gma-abc-reporter-mistakenly-appears-tv-without-pants/3039932001/.
6 History.com editors, "'Nipplegate' Controversy at the Super Bowl XXXVIII Halftime Show," History.com, October 22,2019, https://www.history.com/this-day-in-history/nipplegate-scandal-super-bowl-halftime-show-jackson-timberlake.

Chapter 16 Body Language

1 Mehrabian, A. (1972). *Nonverbal Communication*. New Brunswick: Aldine Transaction.

2 Practical Psychology, "MicroExpressions — Reading Facial Expressions Are Better Than Reading Body Language," YouTube, December 2, 2017, https://www.youtube.com/watch?v=tu1uzG_EBGM&feature=youtu.be.

3 P. Ekman and W. V. Friesen, "Constants Across Cultures in the Face and Emotion," *Journal of Personality and Social Psychology* 17, no. 2 (1971): 124–129.

4 Susan Weinschenk, "Your Hand Gestures Are Speaking for You," *Psychology Today*, September 26, 2012, www.psychologytoday.com/us/blog/brain-wise/201209/your-hand-gestures-are-speaking-you.

5 Linda Talley, Samuel Temple, "How Leaders Influence Followers Through the Use of Nonverbal Communication," *Leadership and Organization Development Journal*, March 2, 2015, www.emerald.com/insight/content/doi/10.1108/LODJ-07-2013-0107/full/html.

6 Amy Cuddy, "Your Body Language May Shape Who You Are," YouTube, TED, October 1, 2012, https://youtu.be/Ks-_Mh1QhMc.

7 James Clear, "How to Be Confident and Reduce Stress in 2 Minutes Per Day," http://jamesclear.com/body-language-how-to-be-confident.

8 Belle Beth Cooper, "The Science Behind Posture and How It Affects Your Brain," LifeHacker, November 13, 2013, lifehacker.com/the-science-behind-posture-and-how-it-affects-your-brai-1463291618.

Chapter 17 Eye Contact

1 David Ludden, "Your Eyes Really Are the Window to Your Soul," *Psychology Today*, December 31, 2015, www.psychologytoday.com/us/blog/talking-apes/201512/your-eyes-really-are-the-window-your-soul.

2 Jennifer Marlow, Eveline van Everdingen, and Daniel Avrahami, "Taking Notes or Playing Games? Understanding Multitasking in Video Communication," *CSCW*, February 27–March 2, 2016, https://dl.acm.org/doi/pdf/10.1145/2818048.2819975.

3 "Making Distance Disappear," *360 Magazine*, 2020, https://www.steelcase.com/research/360-magazine/making-distance-disappear/.

4 Heather Schwedel, "Staring at the Gargoyle on My Screen," *Slate*, December 2, 2019, accessed April 16, 2012, https://slate.com/human-interest/2019/12/video-conferencing-is-the-worst.html.

5 Anne Quito, "We're All Distracted by How Terrible We Look on Video Calls. Here's How to Fix It," *Quartz*, August 22, 2016, https://qz.com/637860/video-call-tips-for-skype-and-facetime-steelcase-researchers-are-solving-your-appearance-barrier-on-video-calls/.

6 Fraser W. Smith and Stephanie Rossit, "Identifying and Detecting Facial Expressions of Emotion in Peripheral Vision," *PLOS One*, May 30, 2018, https://journals.plos.org/plosone/article?id=10.1371/journal.pone.0197160.

Chapter 18 Essentials of VILT Course Design

1 Ryan Hilgemann, "Segmenting Principle," Cognitive Theory of Multimedia Learning website, accessed April 16, 2021, https://sites.google.com/site/cognitivetheorymmlearning/segmenting-principle.

2 Richard E. Mayer, "Segmenting Principle," *Multimedia Learning* (Cambridge University Press: 2009): 175–188, https://www.cambridge.org/core/books/multimedia-learning/segmenting-principle/37240877DDA0362355ADB39936027982.

3 "Reigeluth, Charles," Educational Learning Theorists & Theories website, Northern Arizona University, accessed April 16, 2021, https://sites.google.com/a/nau.edu/educationallearningtheories/home/charles-reigeluth.

Chapter 19 Media and Visuals

1 Cheryl L. Grady, Anthony R. McIntosh, M. Natasha Rajah, and Fergus I. M. Craik. "Neural Correlates of the Episodic Encoding

of Pictures and Words," *PNAS* 95, no. 5 (March 3, 1998): 2703–2708, https://doi.org/10.1073/pnas.95.5.2703.

2 Rachel Gillett, "Why We're More Likely to Remember Content with Images and Video (Infographic)," *Fast Company*, September 18, 2014, https://www.fastcompany.com/3035856/why-were-more-likely-to-remember-content-with-images-and-video-infogr.

3 3M, "Polishing Your Presentation," 1997, http://web.archive.org/web/20001102203936/http%3A//3m.com/meetingnetwork/files/meetingguide_pres.pdf.

Chapter 20 VILT Delivery Preparation

1 Walter B. Cannon, *The Wisdom of the Body* (New York: W.W. Norton & Company, 1932).

2 Katrin Schoenenberg, Alexander Raake, and Judith Koeppe, "Why Are You So Slow? – Misattribution of Transmission Delay to Attributes of the Conversation Partner at the Far-End," *International Journal of Human-Computer Studies* 72, no. 1 5 (May 2014): 477–487, https://doi.org/10.1016/j.ijhcs.2014.02.004.

Chapter 22 Controlling the Virtual Classroom

1 Myrko Thum, "What Is the Present Moment?" MyrkoThum.com, August 31, 2008, https://www.myrkothum.com/what-is-the-present-moment/.

2 Manyu Jiang, "The Reason Zoom Calls Drain Your Energy?" BBC Remote Control, April 22, 2020, www.bbc.com/worklife/article/20200421-why-zoom-video-chats-are-so-exhausting.

Chapter 23 VILT Communication Plan

1 Cisco, "Cisco Annual Internet Report," March 9, 2020, https://www.cisco.com/c/en/us/solutions/collateral/executive-perspectives/annual-internet-report/white-paper-c11-741490.html.

2 Laura Frances Bright, *Consumer Control and Customization in Online Environments: An Investigation into the Psychology of Consumer Choice and Its Impact on Media Enjoyment, Attitude, and Behavioral Intention* (Austin: The University of Texas, 2008), https://repositories.lib.utexas.edu/handle/2152/18054.

3 Robert B. Cialdini, *Influence: The Psychology of Persuasion* (New York: William Morrow and Company, 1993).

Chapter 24   The Fine Art of Engagement

1 Viet Thanh Nguyen, "I Actually Like Teaching on Zoom," *New York Times*, February 15, 2021, https://www.nytimes.com/2021/02/15/opinion/zoom-video-school-teaching.html.

2 BS Morris, P Chrysochou, JD Christensen, JL Orquin, J Barraza, PJ Zak, and P Mitkidis, "Stories vs. Facts: Triggering Emotion and Action-Taking on Climate Change," *Climatic Change* 154 (April 6, 2019): 19–36, https://doi.org/10.1007/s10584-019-02425-6.

3 Paul J. Zak, "Why Your Brain Loves Good Storytelling," *Harvard Business Review*, October 28, 2014, https://hbr.org/2014/10/why-your-brain-loves-good-storytelling.

4 Simona Ondrejkova, "The Neuroscience of Story: How Stories Change Our Brains," *Storius* magazine, June 12, 2020, https://medium.com/storiusmag/the-neuroscience-of-story-how-stories-change-our-brains-7ed955b76f03.

Acknowledgments

Wow, book number thirteen! This was not an easy book to write. It challenged and pushed me out of my comfort zone.

I believed it would take 90 days to finish the manuscript. It took a year. The project may have taken even longer, or possibly ended in failure, had I not had such an incredible team of people around me.

A huge thank you to our Sales Gravy Master trainers and in particular Brad Adams, Beth Maynard, Cynthia Mathis, Jason Eatmon, Jessica Stokes, and Gina Trimarco who embraced virtual training. Your learning, experience, and success working in the virtual classroom are woven into the pages of this book.

I especially want to thank Keith Lubner for adopting virtual training early and inspiring our entire team to reach higher.

I also owe a debt of gratitude to David Monostori, the mastermind behind our virtual training studios, for developing the Virtual Learning Experience Certification and the Sales Gravy "Training Tree."

Likewise, thank you to Trey LaMarr and Ulysses Price, our incredible producers, for playing central roles in helping us perfect virtual training production and developing many of the processes outlined in this book.

As always, I'm so thankful for the Wiley team and all of the support you provide.

Shannon Vargo, thank you for greenlighting this important book. Your encouraging words and kindness inspire me to keep writing. I am grateful for your friendship.

Sally Baker, thank you for all of your support and communication. It means the world knowing that you are always there to help me.

Deborah Schindler, I love working with you more than you can possibly know. You are my rock in the editing phase. Thank you as always for being so flexible.

Christina Verigan, thank you, thank you, thank you for the work you did to shape this book. You made the writing process so much easier and made me look brilliant. You are amazing!

A huge thank you to Mary Lester and Lisa Harris for the unenviable work you did (and do every day) to protect my time and keep me on track. I know that keeping up with me is like herding a pile a feral cats. You make my life easier (though I rarely return the favor), and for that I am grateful.

Abby Lester, you are an incredible and gifted editor. Thank you so much for dropping everything to dig through the pages of this book and find every typo and mistake. We would never have made it to print on time or in such good shape without you.

Finally, my biggest thank you is to my amazing wife, Carrie. Without you, nothing I do is possible.

About the Author

Jeb Blount is the author of 13 books and among the world's most respected thought leaders on sales, leadership, and customer experience.

As a business leader, Jeb has more than 25 years of experience with Fortune 500 companies, small and midsize businesses (SMBs), and startups. His flagship website, SalesGravy.com, is the most visited sales-specific website on the planet.

Through his global training organization, Sales Gravy, Jeb and his team train and advise a who's who of the world's most prestigious organizations.

Jeb's books include:

Fanatical Prospecting Playbook (John Wiley & Sons, 2021)

Virtual Training (John Wiley & Sons, 2021)

Virtual Selling (John Wiley & Sons, 2020)

Inked (John Wiley & Sons, 2020)

Fanatical Military Recruiting (John Wiley & Sons, 2019)

Objections (John Wiley & Sons, 2018)

Sales EQ (John Wiley & Sons, 2017)

Fanatical Prospecting (John Wiley & Sons, 2015)

People Love You: The Real Secret to Delivering a Legendary Customer Experience (John Wiley & Sons, 2013)

People Follow You: The Real Secret to What Matters Most in Leadership (John Wiley & Sons, 2011)

People Buy You: The Real Secret to What Matters Most in Business (John Wiley & Sons, 2010)

Connect with Jeb on LinkedIn, Twitter, Facebook, YouTube, and Instagram. Listen to his Sales Gravy podcast.

To schedule Jeb to speak at your next event, call 1–888–360–2249, email brooke@salesgravy.com or carrie@salesgravy.com, or visit www.jebblount.com. You may email Jeb directly at jeb@salesgravy.com.

Training, Workshops, and Speaking

Sales Gravy offers a comprehensive suite of training programs and workshops for trainers, sales professionals, leaders, account executives, SDRs, account managers, customer service professionals, and channel managers. Our programs include:

- Virtual Learning Experience Train the Trainer Bootcamp
- Virtual Selling Skills
- Sales Negotiation Skills
- Business Outcome Selling (Large and Complex Accounts)
- Mastering Sales Objections
- Sales EQ
- Fanatical Prospecting Bootcamp
- Prospecting Sequencing
- Webchat Sale and Service Bootcamp
- Fanatical Military Recruiting
- Situational Coaching
- Coaching Ultra-High Performance
- Adaptive Mentoring
- Pivotal Leadership Strategies
- The OutBound Leader
- Message Matters
- Spontaneous Selling
- Sales Presentation and Communication Skills
- Business Guidance Selling (cloud, SaaS, IoT)

- Customer Experience Selling (B2C)
- Adaptive Account Management
- Customer EQ
- Adaptive Partnering (channel management)

All training programs are delivered by our certified professional trainers or may be licensed and delivered by your learning and development team. We offer self-directed learning via the Sales Gravy University Platform – https://www.SalesGravy.University – or we can deliver e-learning content to your LMS.

The training media, educational design, and delivery connect with adult learning preferences and are responsive to multigenerational learning styles. We employ an active learning method ology that blends interactive instruction with experiential learning elements and role-playing scenarios to create reference experiences that anchor key concepts and make training stick.

In addition to training, we specialize in developing custom sales onboarding learning paths for new hires and sales playbooks.

For more information, please call 1–844–447–3737, or visit https://www.SalesGravy.com.

Index